La Vita Lunga a Le "Long Life to You"

Ennio and Gina's Love Story

Peter Felix Lieggi

AuthorHouse™
1663 Liberty Drive
Bloomington, IN 47403
www.authorhouse.com
Phone: 833-262-8899

Because of the dynamic nature of the Internet, any web addresses or links contained in this book may have changed since publication and may no longer be valid. The views expressed in this work are solely those of the author and do not necessarily reflect the views of the publisher, and the publisher hereby disclaims any responsibility for them.

Any people depicted in stock imagery provided by Getty Images are models, and such images are being used for illustrative purposes only.
Certain stock imagery © Getty Images.

This book is printed on acid-free paper.

ISBN: 979-8-8230-2818-9 (sc)
ISBN: 979-8-8230-2819-6 (hc)
ISBN: 979-8-8230-2820-2 (e)

Library of Congress Control Number: 2024912194

Print information available on the last page.

Published by AuthorHouse 08/05/2024

authorHOUSE®

For Paul Robert Lieggi

November 8, 1957-August 3, 2024

Dedicated to the memory of my parents, my therapists who helped me when Maggie McVeigh suddenly passed away in 2017. Maggie was my adviser of life and friend since high school. The late Mike "Graz" Graziano, who was instrumental being a good friend from 1979 to 1995, after that we went our separate ways. We kept in touch. And Kevin Kinnevy, my wingman and friend from Saint Anthony High School who passed before his time prior to 2017. It is also dedicated to my parents grandchildren, who loved them Plus the customers who paid our salaries and made the creditors happy by using their merchandise plus food and drink.

To the guys I played football with, Matt Erdie, Bill Ryan, and Donald Montgomery, and my friend Art Tranter, who all passed between 2004 and 2022. Without them, the urge to write about life would not be there. Until the next dimension, old friends, I love you always and forever!

Table of Contents

Introduction

My dad, Ennio, was born on May 30, 1927. Ennio's mom and dad were Rocco Felix Lieggi and Maria Pirone Lieggi. My mom, Gina, was born July 2, 1928, to Mauro Stanislaus Ruberto and Jennie "Giovannina" Cifelli Ruberto. Dad was the grandson of Filomena LaFrancesca Lieggi and Felice Lieggi on his father's side and Giovanni and Angelena Pirone on his mother's side. Mom was the granddaughter of Angelo and Angelena Carnevale-Cifelli on her mother's side and Guiseppe and Albrina Ruberto on her father's side. Mom's mom was born in Lambertville, New Jersey, in 1901; her father was born in Italy in 1900. Dad's mom and dad were born in 1894 and 1887, respectively.

Mom's grandmother passed young in 1905, so Jennie was shipped off to Italy to live with relatives—not by her choice, but by her father's. I loved my grandmother very much, and cried my eyes out when she passed in 1973. Their early life was sketchy, but Mom had two brothers and one sister: Livorno was born in 1922, Rita in 1925, and Guiseppe "Joe" in 1933. Dad had two brothers and one sister as well: Felix in 1920, Antonio "Anthony" in 1923, and Esterina "Esther" in 1935. There were two others who died in the years before 1930, or so Dad had said. The birth certificates and such were in the municipal building in Pettoranello di Molise in the Abruzzi region of Italy. They were born in a house with a midwife. Mom Went up to fifth grade with a diploma and Dad would do his education away from the town.

CHAPTER 1

A Snowy Introduction of More Than Seventy-Four Years

The scene: a village in the mountains, above the town of Isernia, in the Abruzzi region. It was winter when Mom and Dad met in 1941 in the midst of World War II–torn Italy. They met when Dad threw a snowball at her face and hit her on the nose. Dad was a spoiled brat. Mom did a lot of work. Like Dad, she had a farm, but their ways of life were different. Dad went to a private school in Caserta run by priests, but he also wore uniforms to salute Fascists and Nazis. He knew how to march like a *soldat*. He was picked on but got even the hard way, through physical means and by using his brain, like slamming a desk on someone's hands. It was a school for high-income families, and Dad attended along with his first cousin Domenic Pirone.

Fascism started with the rise of Mussolini (Il Duce, as he was called). It was the reason Anthony and Felix Lieggi, Livorno Ruberto, cousins and friends of my mom, and my dad's brothers, left Italy before 1939. It was the depth of the Great Depression, and money was scarce. The men came to America, worked, saved, made money, and sent money home. They left for the American dream. The problem was twofold: Fascism, Nazism, and Socialism took hold of Europe, and soon, in September 1939, the neutrality of war ended for the US. The dream went sour with the bombing of Pearl Harbor on December 7, 1941. Mussolini was a fool, sacrificing a country to be with a man who had no regard for human life. He thought it would be an easy victory—just ask the Poles, the Czechs, the Chinese, and those entombed in the *USS Arizona*! No one learns and no one remembers till they have visited Monte Casino near Naples and Normandy.

Those who left settled in Princeton and Lambertville, New Jersey. My dad was in school, living the life of Riley, Italian style, minding his own business and free from family headaches. His father and brothers would send money back to Italy when they could. It paid for the school and farm till December 7, 1941. Then mail was impossible. Even the letters sent through Grandpop's employer, Albert Einstein, via Switzerland became impossible, as the Fascists got wise and opened the letters. Eventually Dad was not able to go to Caserta; the bombing by American and British forces stopped that. He began working the farm and learning a trade. He also saw the horrors of war.

As the years went by, Mom and Dad got to know each other, and Uncle Gaetano Pirone turned into their chaperone. Dad and Uncle Gaetano went to the mill to make flour, and the two of them met up with my mom and another woman, who disappeared conveniently. The Germans were patrolling, so like a good uncle and nephew, they walked Mom home. You could call that their first date. It was the way to make a connection and begin a romance. The uncle decided then that the two should be together. Soon, the events of real war began on September 10, 1943.

CHAPTER 2

The Realization of War, Accepting Occupation, and Liberation

On the morning of September 10, 1943, at ten minutes past ten in the morning, the bombs fell on the town of Isernia, below Pettoranello di Molise. The Germans were ready. From the town above, both the Wehrmacht and townspeople could see the destruction of a city. When Dad's *nonno* (*grandfather* in Italian) Felice Lieggi, age eighty-four, said he saw black smoke, all Dad's grandfather could say was, "God damn, it's war!" Over ten thousand were dead.

Later, my uncle Felix Lieggi, of the US Army Air Corps, saw how they'd missed the bridge that was the target. He was afraid he had killed his own family; that is why he went there. His squadron carried out the bombing, and like many animosities still, you can't deny it until you've been there. I've been there three times—in 1982, 1998, and August 2006. They know my name, my uncle, and my country. There is a clock in the town that stopped at 10:10. A tour guide showed me what I wanted to know and the sculpture of memorial to the dead. My nieces Rachel and Alexandra saw it at ages twelve and ten, respectively. Even though it might not be a memory for them now, it was for their *zia* Riccardina Ruberto of Isernia, who was in her nineties in 2006. Isernia is still rebuilding. All I can say is *please forgive the Allies who followed orders, in retaliation against Hitler, because of September 1939.*

The Germans saw what would happen to them, and soon they started to disperse and go north to Rome as the British and Americans, under Mark Clark, rolled up the boot. When my father told his grandfather it was the Germans, he said, "Germans? No!" He'd known Germans in America before 1914; they were hardworking people. My great-grandfather had had a stroke, was suffering from dementia, and was bedridden, drinking his wine. He didn't like Hitler, an Austrian.

Mom and Dad's romance continued. During the retreat of the Germans, they left desks, motorcycles, and anything they couldn't bring with them. The Eighth Army of the British came in, and Dad's grandfather proudly said, in not so many words, "I'm an American citizen!" When the letters came, They were coming from America through Switzerland, then to the post office at Pettoranello; they were sent by Einstein's sister. The secretary of Einstein would help, as letters were switched in Switzerland from American postage to Swiss. Switzerland was neutral during the war. The Fascists ended that. Mostly, the Facists trusted noone, this was evident when some men were taken with the German army during the retreat. They had total silence as my parents do now. They remember the Nazis well, and even in America, the Nazis are no better than the KKK and the Fascists. It is unknown if the residents of either Isernia or Pettoranello survived the Nazi introduction to life. They didn't talk freely of it to me, but all I knew was handed down from father to son and mother to son. Most of them are deceased. There are a few left, and we respect their privacy.

CHAPTER 3

The Beginning of the Courtship

My great-aunt Venezia Ruberto-Toto told my father, in not so many words, "Don't cheat on my Jeanette!" Some of the aspects of the war are scarce, as all that remains are letters between my mom and dad between 1946 and 1947, when my mom left Pettoranello first through the port in Naples. My dad worked in the borough hall for the town and was living carefree, as his sister and mother had left for America. The letters were mostly written by Mom; Dad didn't write back much.

The first voyage was simple. Uncle Joe was in first class with Nonna, as he was an American citizen before birth because Grandpop was naturalized before 1930. Nonna Jenny brought Mom, Uncle Joe, and Rita to Hawthorne Avenue to live at Zia Emily Ruberto's house in Princeton before settling at 48 Pine Street. Nonna Maria brought Zia Esterine (Esther) with her before them to the pier in New York. My grandfather took them to the house on Birch Avenue, where they lived with John and Magdelena Leiggi, cousins to Mike Lieggi of Princeton, who served in the Great War for the United States in 1917.

The house on Linden Lane was several years later. Dad had worked for the King Emmanuel II regime before it turned from monarchy to republic, and he continued at age twenty, after the monarchy was dissolved. The problem was he should have stopped working, but no one told him he was now an employee of the new republic. The American embassy sent him to the Italian consulate, then they sent him back to the American embassy—very confusing. It was like playing ping-pong, Roman style. Finally, with the help of US Senator Howard Alexander Smith and a little aid from Einstein, a letter to the State Department got him in. No one knows where the letter is now, but the US allowed his Italian passport.

5

CHAPTER 4

Ennio's Voyage to the New World and His New Adventure

So, the journey began by a troop boat owned by Italy. Dad got seasick and shared a room with at least a dozen guys; it was the best they could do. He came to America and learned a trade he did not want—janitor! With the education he had, he refused to enter the theology school. Bashful and refusing to enter school, he had to settle for working for Uncle Livorno Ruberto, who had returned from the American army, at the Princeton Inn. He was first a dishwasher, and then he began cooking in the kitchen.

Mom and Dad continued to court for a year. She had written him many times, too, before he came to America. He would ride a bicycle for one while Mom sat on the handlebars. Princeton was easy to live in without a car. They took trains from the dinky to Trenton or AC. The date was set for a wedding—July 31, 1948, a Saturday. It would be held on Nassau Street with Father Joe Keenan presiding and relative Joseph Proccacini, who later became a priest in Allentown, New Jersey, as altar boy. Mom and her bridesmaids were ready on Pine Street, while Dad was on Birch Avenue. Saint Paul's Old Church was selected for the ceremony. Domenic Pirone was the best man, and Ann Toto, later Pagliaro, was maid of honor. Ann was a relative of Nonna Jennie, a Cifelli. After the ceremony, the reception was at Mike's Bar on Birch, complete with beer, wine, and sandwiches. Their song was "The Tennessee Waltz," the strangest song for an Italian couple. Following the wedding, they embarked on a honeymoon in Atlantic City. With them at the Lexington Hotel were Uncle Livorno Ruberto and Aunt Jane, his wife. They spent time on the beach and boardwalk. There were no casinos in 1948. They got there by train.

Following the honeymoon, they resided in Princeton. Dad worked, and Mom worked until Joe was born. Dad and Mom lived with Nonno Rocco and Maria Lieggi at Linden Lane. Dad worked for his father, doing lawns like at Einstein's and cooking at Princeton Inn. Mom also worked in Princeton, for Miss Coupeal. Once Joe was born she became a housewife, and the rest is history. They had continuous income but no extracurricular activities except for a club called Roma Eterna and Princeton Italian

American Sportsman Club, but after a while Dad didn't want any part of either—why, only he knows, I can only speculate.

Mom's favorite memory, according to her, is that Einstein once said, "Your father can plant a tree upside down and it will come up right side up; you cannot do that!" All references to Einstein are common knowledge between cousins and goombahs, as Italians were called by the locality. Whether Einstein really helped or not we can only speculate, because these stories have been handed down from generation to generation in postwar Princeton, and unlike today, we took their words for it.

As the summer came, so did Mom's first pregnancy. Dr. Proctor of Princeton Hospital was a busy man, because there were five of us. Of the five children, two would be conceived in Princeton, but all five were born in Princeton. Joe was the first of five. Ennio Jr. came in 1951. Mom had one miscarriage between and Ennio Jr. and Paul. Our sister was stillborn, and I think Mom would have named her Susanna. Another scare in 1956 was rheumatic fever, and we learned Mom was allergic to forms of penicillin. Her other three children were born in Princeton but conceived in Lawrenceville, so we have the best of both worlds.

Saint Paul's and Notre Dame High School were the schools for Joe and J.R., as we called Ennio Jr., and Sister Stella Marie told the boys they could speak Italian in school; they had to speak English. Most other children didn't like others speaking of them in a foreign tongue, I guess. Joe and Ennio Jr. were predominantly raised in Princeton until 1953. After grammar and high school came girls; they were inseparable, going to the Coffee Cup on Lawrence Road. In 1969, Joe was a soldier in the US Air Force: Staff Sergeant,and he got his job done.

Born in 1951, Ennio Jr. was the same as Joe education-wise, but Ennio Jr. was a football player for Notre Dame High with his friends and Domenic Alphonse. His friend Fuzzy Falzone was my coach freshman year, and he loved the games down at the shore—especially the wheel to win cigarettes. Then, one night in 1967, he was in a bad, near-fatal car crash with two young people in the front seat; Junior was in the back seat. So, Junior had a brush with death like Uncle Felix had with a drunk driver. That almost made Dad grieve twice in eight years. The gang of the Coffee Cup got a card for everyone to sign and present to Junior in the hospital. So, he'd had his first car accident, plus a settlement, at age sixteen, graduated senior year, and went into the US Marines after his big brother left for the air force. He finished boot camp on Paris Island, ranked private, did guard duty, and received a US Marine Corps honorable discharge. Like his brother, he engaged in the hospitality industry, and he found his nook as a state employee as a security guard for the NJSP, as the restaurant had pull. Joe also had several other, better, opportunities in the private sector, as well as having his picture taken with US President William Jefferson Clinton at the Excelsior Hotel and receiving an honor from the White House.

I was the athlete, the larger-than-life member of the family in the sports section, as evident as a picture. Paul, born in 1957, was a Saint Ann's and Notre Dame graduate, a Drew University and John Marshall Law School graduate, and a prominent lawyer in the city of Chicago. He was better athlete than me in Lawrence Township: basketball for Saint Ann's, football for Notre Dame, and baseball in Little League and Babe Ruth for Lawrence Township. He was an exceptional student, *numero uno* of the family—the first to go to a real college and excel because he hit the books earning it. Anna was real smart and could have gone to a good college in Boston, but she chose to stay in Mercer County with her boyfriend, friends, and family. We were both Saint Ann's and Notre Dame graduates, as well as Rider College students, but the difference was that I finished Rider. She didn't because she chose love and marriage instead. I finished Rider College in 1997 in addition to Mercer County Community College in 1991. Anna chose real estate but also helped as a server at the restaurant. Paul worked at the restaurant sparingly; his career was always first to Dad, so he became the lawyer of his style of law. He was the pride and joy of Mom, too, and she never forgot when he spent his first Thanksgiving alone, away from family, because Mom and Dad didn't have the money to fly him home from Chicago for the blessed family event. Dad didn't open for Turkey Day at that time.

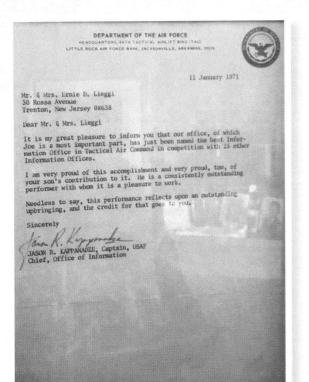

DEPARTMENT OF THE AIR FORCE
HEADQUARTERS, 64TH TACTICAL AIRLIFT WING (TAC)
LITTLE ROCK AIR FORCE BASE, JACKSONVILLE, ARKANSAS, 72076

11 January 1971

Mr. & Mrs. Ernie D. Lieggi
30 Rossa Avenue
Trenton, New Jersey 08638

Dear Mr. & Mrs. Lieggi

It is my great pleasure to inform you that our office, of which Joe is a most important part, has just been named the best Information Office in Tactical Air Command in competition with 25 other Information Offices.

I am very proud of this accomplishment and very proud, too, of your son's contribution to it. He is a consistently outstanding performer with whom it is a pleasure to work.

Needless to say, this performance reflects upon an outstanding upbringing, and the credit for that goes to you.

Sincerely

JASON R. KAPPANADZE, Captain, USAF
Chief, Office of Information

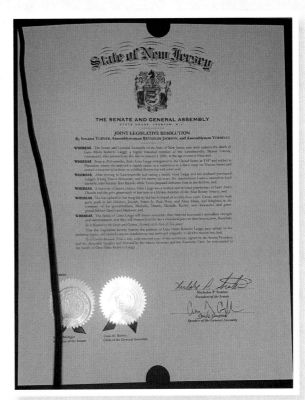

State of New Jersey

THE SENATE AND GENERAL ASSEMBLY
STATE HOUSE, TRENTON, N.J.

JOINT LEGISLATIVE RESOLUTION

By Senator TURNER, Assemblywoman REYNOLDS-JACKSON, and Assemblyman VERRELLI

WHEREAS, The Senate and General Assembly of the State of New Jersey note with sadness the death of Gina Maria Ruberto Lieggi, a highly esteemed member of the Lawrenceville, Mercer County, community, who passed from this life on January 3, 2023, at the age of ninety-four; and,

WHEREAS, Born in Pietrasticla, Italy, Gina Lieggi immigrated to the United States in 1947 and settled in Princeton, where she enjoyed a superb career as a seamstress in a dress shop on Nassau Street and earned a reputation of acclaim as a skilled dressmaker and tailor; and,

WHEREAS, After growing to Lawrenceville and raising a family, Gina Lieggi and her husband purchased Lieggi's Ewing Manor restaurant, and for twenty-six years, this consummate hostess catered to loyal clientele, who became dear friends, while Ennio prepared delicious fare in the kitchen; and,

WHEREAS, A survivor of breast cancer, Gina Lieggi was a faithful and devoted parishioner of Saint Ann's Church and she gave generously of her time as a lifetime member of the Altar Rosary Society; and,

WHEREAS, She was upheld in her long life by her late husband of seventy-four years, Ennio, and she took great pride in her children, Joseph, Ennio Jr., Paul, Peter, and Anna Maria, and delighted in the company of her grandchildren, Michelle, Danielle, Michelle, Rachel, and Alexandra, and great-grandchildren Derek and Madison; and,

WHEREAS, The family of Gina Lieggi will always remember their beloved matriarch's boundless strength and determination, and they will forever hold for her a cherished place in their hearts; now, therefore,

Be It Resolved by the Senate and General Assembly of the State of New Jersey:

That this Legislature hereby honors the memory of Gina Maria Ruberto Lieggi, pays tribute to her enduring legacy, and extends sincere condolences and profound sympathy to all who mourn her; and,

Be It Further Resolved, That a duly authenticated copy of this resolution, signed by the Senate President and the Assembly Speaker, and attested by the Senate Secretary and the Assembly Clerk, be transmitted to the family of Gina Maria Ruberto Lieggi.

Nicholas P. Scutari
President of the Senate

Craig J. Coughlin
Speaker of the General Assembly

... Menzger
... of the Senate

Dana M. Burley
Clerk of the General Assembly

NEW JERSEY SENATE

SHIRLEY K. TURNER
SENATOR, 15TH DISTRICT
1230 PARKWAY AVENUE
SUITE 103
EWING, NJ 08628
WEBSITE www.senatorturner.com

TEL (609) 323-7239
FAX (609) 323-7693
E-MAIL senturner@njleg.org

VICE CHAIR
EDUCATION COMMITTEE

MEMBER
STATE GOVERNMENT, WAGERING,
TOURISM & HISTORIC PRESERVATION COMMITTEE
SENATE ECONOMIC GROWTH COMMITTEE

COMMISSIONER
EDUCATION COMMISSION OF THE STATES

January 7, 2023

Family of Gina Maria Ruberto Lieggi
c/o Brenna Funeral Home, Immordino Chapel
1799 Klockner Road
Hamilton, NJ 08619

Dear Lieggi Family,

Please accept my heartfelt condolences upon the passing of Gina Maria Ruberto Lieggi and my deepest sympathy for the loss of yet another pillar of the Lieggi Family. I write this letter to add my voice to the many expressions of sympathy and support that you are now receiving from your large and loving family.

Mrs. Lieggi is being remembered as a woman of strength who lovingly provided constant and unwavering support to her late husband Ennio and her beloved children and grandchildren. Blessed with a warm nature, Mrs. Lieggi was the heart and face of Lieggi's Ewing Manor restaurant for twenty-six years. During that time, she, and her husband Ennio infused Ewing Township with delicious food, impeccable service, and lifelong memories. She was an extraordinary individual, and I am certain that she appreciated her family's support and presence during her later years.

Mrs. Lieggi leaves this life as a cherished wife, a devoted mother, a loving grandmother, and an accomplished businesswoman. Again, please accept my deepest sympathies for your loss and the accompanying resolution to honor the life and memory of Mrs. Gina Maria Ruberto Lieggi. If I can assist you in any way, please do not hesitate to call on me.

Sincerely,

Shirley K. Turner
Senator – 15th District

Enclosure

Army of the United States

Honorable Discharge

This is to certify that

LIVORNO M RUBERTO 32 366 388 TECHNICIAN FOURTH GRADE
SERVICE BATTERY 113 TH FIELD ARTILLERY BN
Army of the United States

is hereby Honorably Discharged from the military service of the United States of America.

This certificate is awarded as a testimonial of Honest and Faithful Service to this country.

Given at SEPARATION CENTER FORT DIX NEW JERSEY
Date 18 OCTOBER 1945

Received in the Clerks Office of the County of Mercer on the 23rd day of Oct A.D. 1945 at 9:45 o'clock in the afternoon, and recorded in Book 7 of DISCHARGES for said County on page 98

W.B. H. Ren Clerk

J H GUNTER
MAJOR, INFANTRY

"What, therefore, God hath joined together let no man put asunder." *Matthew xix. 6.*

This Certifies that
Gina Ruberto
and
Ennio Lieggi
were united by me
in the bonds of
Holy Matrimony
According to the Rite of the
Holy Catholic Church

at St. Paul's Church

on the 31st day

of July in the

year of Our Lord, 1948

Signed Joseph S. Keenan

Witnesses

Maid of Honor:
Anna Toto
Best Man: Domenic
Pirone
Bridesmaids: Elvira Rosso
Rita Ruberto
Groomsmen: Vincenzo Pirone
Umberto Ruberto

Certificate of Baptism

Church of
St Johns
Lambertville N.J.

— This is to Certify —

That Jennie Cifelli
Child of Angelo Cifelli
and Angelina Carunnola
born in Lambertville N.J.
on the 24" day of June 1901
was Baptized
on the 7" day of July 1901
According to the Rite of the Roman Catholic Church
by the Rev. William H Lynch
the Sponsors being Thomas Phillips
Maria Rossi

as appears from the Baptismal Register of this Church.

Dated Apr 29 1941

Rev C. J. Farran
Pastor

NO. 314 F. J. REILEY CO. INC. N.Y.

AIRPLANE RIDE

RACHEL MARTINEZ
NAME

TRENTON MERCER CO.
AIRPORT

CESSNA 175 / N7018M
AIRPLANE/N-NUMBER

JUNE 1st 1997
DATE

PETE WEBSTER
PILOT

INTERNATIONAL ORGANIZATION OF LICENSED WOMEN PILOTS

The Lieggi Family of Lieggi's Ewing Manor, Trenton
is presented with a plaque by Susan Fajgier, Special
Events Assistant for the March of Dimes, for
supporting the 1986 Dining Out fundraiser.

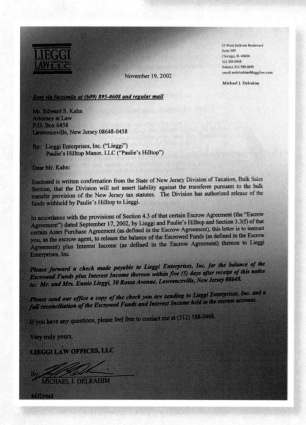

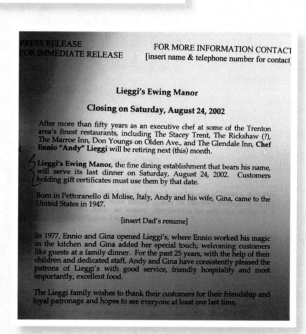

Document 1 — Alien Registration Statement

ALIEN REGISTRATION
Name *Giovannina Ruberto*
No. 6 244 368

STATEMENT OF FACTS FOR PREPARATION OF PETITION

(1) My full, true, and correct name is *Giovannina Ruberto*

(2) My present place of residence is *48 Pine, Princeton, NJ*

(3) My occupation is *Housewife*   (4) I am *59* years old.

(5) I was born on *June 22, 1901* in *Lambertville*

(6) My personal description is as follows: Sex *female*; color of eyes *brown*; color of hair *gray*; height *5'5"*; weight *124* pounds; visible distinctive marks *none*

(7) I am (am not) married; the name of my present husband is *Stanislao Mauro Ruberto, Italy*
we were married on *Aug. 27*, *19—*, at *Pettoranello di Molise, Italy*

(8) I have *4* children; and the name, sex, place and date of birth, and present place of residence of each of said children is living, are as follows:

Name	Sex	Place Born	Date Born	Now Living At
Liverno	M	*Pettoranello*	May 2, 1922	Princeton, NJ
Rita	F	do	Aug 28, 1925	do
Gina	F	Italy	Sep 2, 1928	Lawrenceville, NJ
Giuseppe	M		Dec 3, 1930	U.S. Army

(11) I have resided continuously in the United States of America since *Mar 11, 1947*

Document 2 — White House Letter

THE WHITE HOUSE
WASHINGTON

November 21, 2023

Mr. Peter Felix John Lieggi
Princeton, New Jersey

Dear Mr. Lieggi,

Thank you for your letter and for sharing such a deeply personal story.

While everyone's battle with cancer is different, the First Lady and I—and our entire family—understand that pain. You are not alone. Nearly everyone knows someone who has had cancer or who is fighting to beat it. We often meet them as we travel the country and, like you, they share their own story of hurt, struggle, and hope.

I am committed to ending cancer as we know it—for the lives we have lost and the lives we can save. That is why the First Lady and I supercharged the Cancer Moonshot. We set ambitious new goals to reduce the death rate from cancer by at least 50 percent over the next 25 years, and improve the experience of people and their families living with and surviving cancer. My Administration also created a special Federal agency called the Advanced Research Projects Agency for Health, ARPA-H, which will invest billions of dollars to deliver breakthrough cures for deadly diseases like cancer.

As we forge ahead to achieve this goal with hope in our hearts, please know that the First Lady and I will keep you and your loved ones in our thoughts and prayers.

Sincerely,

[signature]

Document 3 — Tax Form

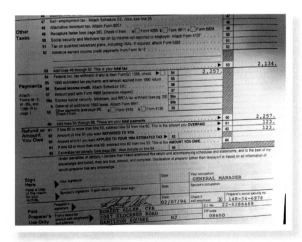

Document 4 — Refunding Bond & Release

DOCKET NO.: 23-00130

STATE OF NEW JERSEY
MERCER COUNTY SURROGATE COURT

IN THE MATTER OF THE ESTATE OF:
GINA MARIA LIEGGI
a/k/a GINA LIEGGI, DECEASED

REFUNDING BOND & RELEASE

KNOW ALL MEN BY THESE PRESENTS, THAT I, PETER F. LIEGGI, of 3839 Quakerbridge Road, in the Township of Hamilton, County of Mercer, State of New Jersey, hereinafter known as the *Obligor*, am held and firmly bound unto JOSEPH R. LIEGGI, Executor of the Estate of Gina Maria Lieggi a/k/a Gina Lieggi, and JOSEPH R. LIEGGI, Trustee of the Gina Lieggi Family Trust under Last Will dated December 30, 1985, both of 8324 Holiday Drive, Sherwood, AR 72129 hereinafter known as the *Obligee*, in the sum of **Fifty Thousand Dollars and No Cents ($50,000.00)** lawful money of the United States of America, to be paid to the *Obligee* or to *Obligee's* Attorney, *Obligee's* successors in office or assigns; for which payment well and truly to be made I bind myself, and my heirs, executors and administrators, firmly by these presents.

THE CONDITION OF THE ABOVE OBLIGATION is such, that whereas, the Obligor has received from the *Obligee* cash in the amount of Fifty Thousand Dollars and No Cents ($50,000.00).

AND IN CONSIDERATION THEREFOR, the *Obligor* has released and forever discharged, and by these presents, does release and forever discharge the *Obligee* from all claims and demands whatsoever on account of or in respect to the estate and testamentary trust of the said deceased, and of *Obligor's* interest therein;

The *Obligor* is a beneficiary of the above named testamentary Family Trust, which is the legatee of the above named Estate, and if any part of the whole of such legacy shall at any time hereafter appear to be wanting to discharge any debt or debts, legacy or legacies, which the said executor or administrator may not have other assets to pay, the *Obligor* will return said legacy or such part thereof as may be necessary for the payment of the said debts, or for the payment of a proportional part of the said legacies.

Then the above obligation to be void, or else to be and remain in full force and virtue.

If more than one person executes the within instruments, then words used in the singular shall be considered to include the plural, and wherever herein any particular gender is used it shall be inclusive of the masculine, feminine and neuter gender, where the text so requires.

SIGNED, SEALED AND DELIVERED
IN THE PRESENCE OF

Rakhi Chandhok
Witness *Rakhi Chandhok*

[signature]
PETER F. LIEGGI, Beneficiary

for 1   Breast of Chicken Parmigiana

a 4 oz breast of chicken
2 sliced of Mozzarella cheese
1 cup plain breaded crumbled
1 cup flower
1 cup egg wash
2 cups Tomato Sauce - Ragu - (see thereof,
2 table spoon of oil
     some grated cheese pecorino Romano

~~But 1 to give aluminum pan the fire adding~~
~~oil and with the~~ Breaded the breast of
Chicken - (pass thru a flower - egg wash a thru
Bread Crumbs) put a aluminum pan too on
the fire until it feel hot put cooked the
Chicken for 4 to 5 minute in each side to a
golden Brown. Remove from the fire putting
in a flat pan - cover with one spoon of tomato
Sauce cover with Sliced Mozzarella cheese adding
little more tomato Sauce on Top. spurted grated
cheese. and Baked them in a oven at 375 for
10 to 12 minute until the cheese is melting.
Server on the plate with little Tomato Sauce.

       Breast of chicken princess for 2

2 - 4 oz breast of chicken
½ lb fresh asparagus (large)
8 sliced Fontina or Mozzarella cheese
½ cup of olive oil or veg oil
2 whole eggs - table grated Parmigian cheese)
1 cup of flower
1 spoon of chopped parsley (if you have)
½ tea spoon salt a ½ tea spoon white peppers -

Flat the breast of chicken thin, butter
the eggs in a bell. add mixed in chopped
parsley, salt & peppers -
Boil or steamed di asparagus (if you have
a peeler peeled the back part of asparagus not
too soft and 6 me long. after cooked cooled them off.
Out a Aluminum Pan of the stove with
medium flame, without oil pass the breast chicken in the
flower (shake the excess flower) drop the breast in
the egg mixed and soon the oil is hot (but not
too hot) put the breast in it cooked for 5 to 6 minute
on each side - until gold on both side - layer in
Baking sheet pan put 6 to 7 asparagus on top

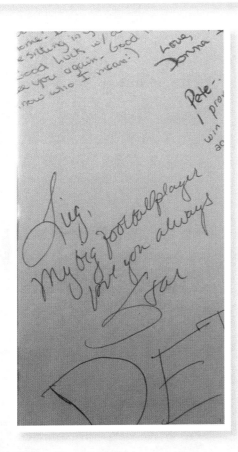

Sig,
My big football player
love you always
Star

WILLIAM J. RYAN
2125 WINDROW
~~26 BURR~~ DRIVE
PRINCETON, NJ. 08540

Aug. 23, 2017

Dear Peter,
     Thank you, really thank you for the
Mass today for Bill. You are a
good friend of Bill's also. Your letter
is very thoughtful. I remember
No. 63 and the formidable front
two. I watched all of your home
games & some on the road. They
were good games & good year. It's
easy to understand the bonding
and its permanency. I am
sharing your letter with Patricia &
Peter.
     May God bless you Peter. Billy
will always be with us.
       Sincerely & gratefully,
       Bill Ryan Sr.
My high school playing number was
59 - Left guard!

I appreciated the years of service, etc and ... attention ... have given to "our table". There will never be another place like Luigi's again. Your Restaurant was one of the best in the area... and your family was also one of the best. We will miss you all, but be happy and healthy and enjoy...

With much love
to all. Tina

Dearest Gino, J.R., Peter and family:

They say that all good things must come to an end. For me family and myself it is the end of good food, fine dining at your beautiful establishment, and seeing the good friends that we all have become! We will dearly miss you and all of your kind faces! We wish you the very best on your new endeavors and all the happiness life has to offer to you and your family!

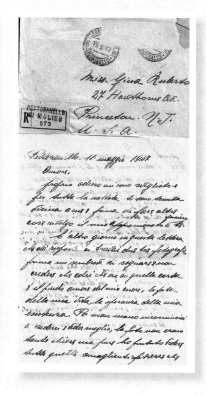

Miss Gina Ruberto
27 Hawthorne Ave.
Princeton. N.J.
U.S.A.

Pettoranello 11 maggio 1947

Amore,

stasera adesso mi sono svegliato e per tutta la nottata io sono sempre sterina a ... prima di farsi altro cosa rivolgo il mio appuntamento a te.

L'altro giorno in questa lettera che ho risposto ... trovai due tue fotografie firma un membro di squarzava mai credere che colei che ora su quella carta è il fondo amore del mio cuore, la fata della mia vita, la speranza della mia esistenza. Poi man mano incomincia a vedere sempre meglio, la foto non erano tanto chiare ma pure ho puntato tutte quelle somiglienze, e però che ...

Princeton 17 luglio 1947

Unico mio conforto

Non mi dispiace se devi Tornare in italia perché io amo a te e vengo dove te sarai io ti lo voluto dire non crede che vuoi rimanere in italia quanto la tuo famiglia e tutto qua io sono sempre coi vostri ordini dove te mi dici io dove come mai amore o poco affetto verso di te se io ti ho scritto di voglio prendere la carta cittadina e mi hai detto di no devi sapere tesoro che ne anche la morte più farmi dimenticare di te io non posso mai dimenticare del mio e soltanto Ermio non dirmi più che io non ti amo che mi arreghi tanto dobbre e specialmente lettima

Miss Gina Ruberto

22

O dolce sposa...

Oggi sono ricevuto due lettere una portando la
data dell'11 e l'altra 14 mi dici di averne
mandata un altra il 9 ma io non le sono ricevuto.
Amore mi perdonerai se ti lo fatto piangere me non
sarò io stato far farti piangere che ti ho sentito
così ma è stato solo per farti sapere che...
più persona i giorni e più il mio cuore palpita
d'amore tanto che non so se ter così come...
di averti fatto le permanente come già ti ho fatto noto
in una precedente io l'ho sapeta tramite altre
persone che te hai scritto e non più me... immagina
che cosa provai, le tue fotografie non le sono ricevute
non so se sono fino che non l'ai rispedite...
ma una sola cosa che se vengono mi dicono che sei...
...ricevute le lettere che...
...non ti offendermi ma come te hai agito e
continui ed agire così fa sospettare e ciò che dici
nella lettera non è altro che ... Mi dici che
sei stata solo una volta a cinema ed io te detto che se
ci sei stata e che c'è... Andrei ancora distesa sott... e se
...fortuna che venisse te lo proverò...

Princeton 14 Aprile 1947

Tesoro del mio cuore.

Sono ricevuto appena 2 lettera da te e ora ti
scrivo perché non posso stare un giorno senza scri-
vere al mio Amore. Tesoro ieri sera siamo venuto
a trovare tua Madre e tuo Padre e stanno tutti
bene e da ieri sera sto un po più contento che tua
tua Madre mi disse che ai scritto che le carte non
ancora ti hanno date che devono cercare prima
informazione a Roma e mi disse che te hai
scritto che per il soldato c'è tempo ancora fino ad
Agosto e sono rimasto un po contento e a me non
mi dicevi nulla soltanto che per le carte non se
ne parla io ti scrivo di farmi sapere cosa fai per le
carte e te non mi rispondi non mi fai sapere nulla
mi fai stare sempre dispiaciuto io ti ho scritto che...
quante lettere e te pensi che io non ti scrivo io ti
scrivo 2 3 volte la settimana

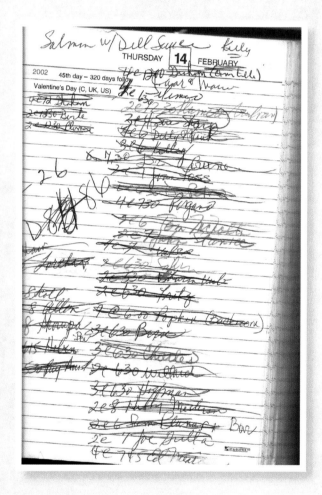

AMERICA

THE LAST BEST HOPE

Welcome To Lieggi's

Our menu has been carefully planned to allow us to offer you our best. Everything we serve is freshly cooked. Good food takes time to prepare and so we invite you to enjoy our cocktails and appetizers in a leisurely manner as you will find that you will not be rushed, but rather encouraged to relax and rediscover the pleasure that really good food and friends can impart.

Monday, Dec. 30, 2002

Dear Comare & Compare,

We were so glad to see you again and visit with us last Thursday. Thank you for the wine — we will certainly enjoy it.

It was a pleasant surprise to have Patino Paul, Mary Ellen, & Danielle visit also, even Rachel. We had such a nice afternoon and wished it could have been even longer. There never seems to be enough time, especially when we don't see each other often. Hopefully, we can visit again when they come again the next time. We're so glad the Patino's law firm is increasing and he's doing so well.

Wishing you a healthy and Happy New Year.

Love,
Comare & Compare
Ann & Phil

Dear Patino Peter,

We certainly missed you last week and sorry you couldn't come, but we understand. I want to thank you for the most beautiful godmother Christmas card you sent me. It was very thoughtful of you and I appreciate it.

Happy & healthy New Year,

Love, Patina Ann

---

lived here before me had bought his own leather chair & the one that was in the room was put in storage — Well — they don't really keep things in storage for long — lack of adequate space — So it probably ended up in another apt. But I have the foot stool that goes w/ the chair so the manager is trying to get me a chair that matches the foot stool.

Oh I finally made tomato sauce today — it came out pretty good. The meatballs didn't come so good though — I think I used too many eggs for the amount of meat I had — but they still tasted good. Came out sort like Wilma's — not quite round. Oh well — practice makes perfect.

But I've been eating good — haven't had any real problems cooking at all — just the time it takes to clean up. I'm tempted to go out and get a dishwasher (not the mechanical one — the human one — I figure a blonde to do my dishes would be real nice.)

I also had a phone put in — but it won't be working til Tuesday (I hope!), the

27

Baccala Soup alla Lieggi

(This recipe I learned from my grandmother Filomena. Its my
favorite course of our traditional family Christmas Eve dinner.)

Ingredients:

1/4 cup of olive oil
3 medium white onions (large dice)
2 medium leeks (sliced large)
4 medium celery stalks (inside w/leaves) (sliced)
2 tablespoons garlic (chopped fine)
1 tablespoon crushed red pepper
2 tablespoons oregano
1 tablespoon ground black pepper
2 tablespoons parsley stalks (chopped fine)
2-3 lbs of imported baccala cut into pieces
4 medium white potatoes (large dice)
1 28 oz can crushed San Marzano tomatoes
4 quarts of water
Salt & additional ground black pepper to taste

...is dish, you need to soak the baccala overnight in
...sove days, changing the water every 8 to 12 hours.

...ep soup pot on the stove over a medium flame for
...approximately one minute, then add the olive oil
...s, celery and leeks to the pot and saute until soft
(approximately 5 minutes)

...ey, crushed red pepper, oregano and ground black
...auté for approximately 1-2 minutes, then add the
baccala.

...e to sauté for 35 minutes and then add tomatoes.
Bring tomatoes to boil and then add the water.

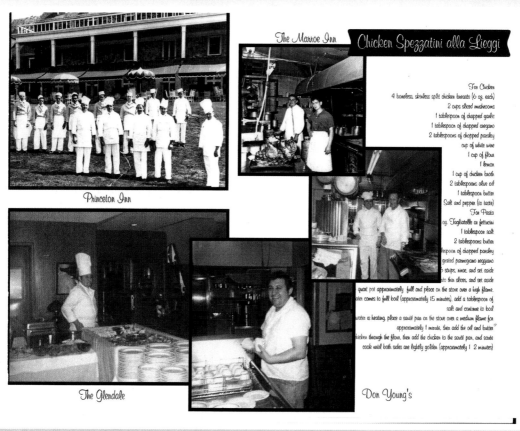

The Marroe Inn

Chicken Spezzatini alla Lieggi

For Chicken
4 boneless, skinless split chicken breasts (6 oz. each)
2 cups sliced mushrooms
1 tablespoon of chopped garlic
1 tablespoon of chopped oregano
2 tablespoons of chopped parsley
cup of white wine
1 cup of flour
1 lemon
1 cup of chicken broth
2 tablespoons olive oil
1 tablespoon butter
Salt and pepper (to taste)

For Pasta
oz. Tagliatelle or fettucini
1 tablespoon salt
2 tablespoons butter
...lespoon of chopped parsley
...grated parmigiano reggiano
...o strips, rinse, and set aside
...nto thin slices, and set aside
...quart pot approximately full and place on the stove over a high flame.
...ater comes to full boil (approximately 15 minutes), add a tablespoon of
salt and continue to boil
...water is heating, place a sauté pan on the stove over a medium flame for
approximately 1 minute, then add the oil and butter
...chicken through the flour, then add the chicken to the sauté pan, and sauté
cook until both sides are lightly golden (approximately 1-2 minutes)

Princeton Inn

The Glendale

Don Young's

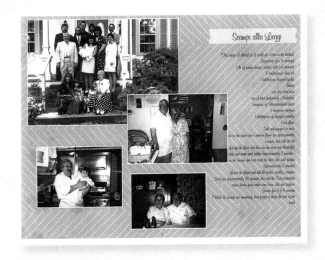

Trentonian Photo By STEVE MERVISH

EWING MILESTONE — Lieggi's Manor House in Ewing Township is marking its 10th anniversary. The owners, Gina and Ennio (Andy) Lieggi (right), receive the township's Meritorious Achievement Award from Mayor Steven Elliott (second from right) and Neil Wesley, chairman of Ewing's Economic Development Committee.

---

or visit came on a Friday, and by 10 p.m., we were about the only ones left in what had been a packed dining room. "Dallas," apparently can draw people from a restaurant as easily as the Cowboys.

"Packed" at Lieggi's means 50 to 60 diners. That may change soon. The proprietor has spruced up the large porch at the entrance and soon may finish it to provide more than 40 additional seats. "If business keeps up and mortgage rates go down, we'll do it," Lieggi reports. "We've had to turn people away most Saturdays and on New Year's Eve we served more than 200 dinners."

Otherwise, it is the same old comfortable L-shaped room. The red napkins, the white cloths over red ones, the paneled walls and soft spotlights from acoustical ceiling, the slightly-loud jukebox playing mostly Sinatra records, the old friends you inevitably run into there, the table filled with women exchanging gifts after dinner (maybe they couldn't get together at Christmastime).

Lieggi's family update is that wife, Gina, now is a full-time hostess, while son Junior, an ex-waiter, runs the bar and has decided to make it a career. The oldest son has become the banquet manager at the Regency Hotel in Dallas; son Paul is a senior in law school who still helps out when he is free, while Peter, who also works at the restaurant, is a Mercer CCC student who hopes to major in business at Villanova.

verall, there seems to have increase in most dishes over years. A filet mignon went $12.90, broiled lobster tails free veal and mushrooms Marsala costs to $10.90. Baked stuffed mushroom appetizer, is the same $5.00 it was Most fish entrees are $9.90, as that may be the best in town. Sal always-fresh vegetables come with side orders of special vegeta available.

One of the evening's spec just flown in from Florida. Doub couldn't resist. Perhaps I shou large ones all tasted of the le were packed. "They cost me $5 can't make anything on them. I have them now and then to plea my " Fearless Dining Companion Linguini alla Genovese and a la shells and mushroom caps that wer the tongue and down on the pa

---

Lieggi's closes, an era ends

A couple of folks from the restaurant business have yielded to the weight of the years and have sold their place to new owners. It is truly the end of an era. The fine dining crowd will truly miss them.

Ennio "Andy" Lieggi and Gina, his wife of 54 years (and counting happily), closed Lieggi's Ewing Manor on West Upper Ferry Road on Aug. 24 after a highly successful run of 25 years.

There was always something mysterious, private, secluded, perhaps even above-the-crowd about the historic old mansion that sits like a grande dame high off the road in a stand of sheltering trees probably older than the great restaurant itself.

ARNOLD ROPEIK

Because I was a bit gimpy at the time and couldn't get around town, the Lieggis and their daughter Anna had graciously come to our house and were honored guests in our living room. Sitting next to each other and holding hands like young lovers, this beautiful senior Italian couple will tell you that "sometimes people were afraid to walk in to have dinner at the restaurant because they thought it was some kind of a private club."

Sure, there was always a smallish, finely drawn sign down on West Upper Ferry, but it was understated and non-neon. Really, you just sort of had TO KNOW where Lieggi's was.

Andy and Gina bought the historic 19th-century building in 1976 from Mary Marks and opened for business in 1977. Records show it was an eating place even before Marks' time and was once called the Bloomingrove Inn of Ewing. Before my time, right?

The Lieggis came to America in 1947 from the little town of Petronello, Italy, now a sister city to Princeton Township because so many Italian families from Petronello have settled there. Andy and Gina married in 1948 and Andy began to find work in the area as a cook and then soon as a master or executive chef. He started at the Princeton Inn and put in time in such noted eating spots as The Rickshaw, Marroe Inn, Don Youngs, The Glendale, the Stacy Trent Hotel and others.

But Andy was very good at what he did and he sensed it. He grew tired of having people say they came to where he was working because of HIS dishes. Why not find a place of his own? After all, he reasoned, he was a chef and king of his kitchen.

Lieggi's Ewing Manor was the answer. It wasn't always easy and the entire family became in-

volved. The Lieggis raised five children, four boys, Joseph, Ennio Jr., Paul, Peter and their daughter Anna. Peter, J.R. and Anna became stalwarts and part of the history of the place. Anna helped greatly with this story as she did in the restaurant.

Andy was always busy in the kitchen. Ah, but Gina, who had progressed from an Old World housewife and mother to become a talented and caring hostess was "out front" day in and day out. She took reservations, greeted people at the door, saw them to their tables, visited with them, listened to them and turned all of them into friends and extended family.

For years, Friday nights at Lieggi's became a sort of combined reunion for those who held Trenton High School and Cathedral High School dear. Everybody knew each other. It was good food, good wine and lots of love.

"The years flew past. It was work but it was fun. We were proud of what we were doing," Gina said quietly, the sweet smile of memory written on her lovely face.

Beloved Spouse, always looking for new recipes, asked Andy if he cooked by written formula or just used a spoonful of this, a spoonful of that. He put his 75-year-old head back and laughed.

"It's not written down. It's up here in my head. I used no spoons. I used my hands so I could truly feel the meal. I bought and butchered the meat to order. Nothing pre-cut. Much better that way," he smiled, wiping away a small tear of joy.

"You know, we did not make a formal announcement of our closing because I was afraid to be swarmed. As it was, just the word of mouth brought out many people, all dear friends. Your column will help us," Gina said.

So, what are they going to do with their free time? Well, it won't always be free. Andy would love to add his expertise on making soups and gravies and special sauces for someone in this epicurean locale so famous for its Italian foods.

And the Lieggis say they are planning a cookbook, filled with all those recipes which will finally find their way to immortality.

Lieggi's restaurant may be gone, but the tastes will linger on. To this loving couple, as they say in Italian:

La vita lunga a le . . . long life to you.

Arnold Ropeik is senior editor of The Times.

Italian cooking and warm hospitality are on the menu at Lieggi's in Ewing

EWING — Gina Lieggi was "just a housewife," she said, during the greater part of her husband's career as a chef. "I spent many days and nights alone, raising our four sons and daughter, while Andy (Ennio) was working.

"It was lonely at Easter, New Year's and most of the holidays because he was always cooking," she said. "But it's not lonely any more!"

Now that the children are grown and gainfully employed three of the five work full time at Lieggi's) Gina has taken up residence as the overseer of the restaurant, and as her husband's greatest fan.

"Andy has been in this country for 45 years, and has been cooking for that long. He is one of the best chefs anywhere," she said.

"He had been studying engineering in Abruzzi, Italy, but did some cooking at home and while he was away at school," she explained. When he first came to this country he worked with my brother, Chef Ruberto, at the Princeton Inn. That was 1947.

AFTER THE Princeton Inn, Andy Lieggi accepted a job as head chef at the Rickshaw in Cherry Hill. But the long hours he was working at the restaurant, combined with the long commute, was exhausting. So in 1972 Andy agreed to head up the kitchen when his brother bought a restaurant in Ewing Township, the Glendale Inn.

After a few years there, and a few at the Golden Goose in Hamilton Township, opportunity knocked. Mary Marks' restaurant in West Trenton was for sale, and the Lieggis were ready for a place of their own.

"She closed on New Year's Eve of 1976, and we opened in January 1977," Gina Lieggi said. "And Andy has never stopped. Every day he thinks of a different dish, he has different ideas, he likes to do it and he never gives up."

In addition to the regular menu, there are four to six daily specials available, both at lunch and dinner. Recent selections were spaghetti (a ruso (with chicken livers), fettuccine Puttanesca, spaghetti and meatballs, fettuccine and broccoli, Salade Nicoise, fresh snapper and shad and roe.

"Andy doesn't use cookbooks, he makes up most of the dishes," Gina Lieggi said. "And I like everything,

Photo by Stan Brick

Owner and chef Ennio Lieggi puts the finishing touches on a plate of his special Spezzatina of Chicken.

of chicken, sliced eggplant, fontina cheese and tomato sauce.

"I think that on Saturday nights someone at every table orders one," she said.

AS MUCH AS her husband enjoys his work in the kitchen, Gina Lieggi

AT A GLANCE

Lieggi's
Ewing Manor

30

In Memory Of
Gina M. Lieggi
1928-2023

Mom, on a Sunday of the New Year 2023, you passed away in Greenwood House, forty nine days after your husband Ennio, " Andy " Lieggi, Sr.

On that day me, your daughter Anna, JR., your grandchildren, Michelle, Rachel, and Alexandra gave you last rites, unordained though it may have been. You deserved the prayers of "Our Father, Hail Mary, Glory Be, Thou I walk into the shadow of death, I fear no evil". Your two great grandchildren were there to send you off into a new life in Christ.

One year later Mom, You are missed, loved, remembered and like Tom Carter's Cantor Angela sang Ave Maria, you are appreciated by your family for all you did for us.

Rest well Mom, rest well with Dad.

Love, your son,
Peter Lieggi

County — Honoring veterans
Woodstown to stage parade on 4th of July
Page A-3

Sports — Rock-solid competitor
Pierce named Player of Year in boys track
Page B-1

Inside
Today's forecast: Mostly cloudy, cool
Details, page A-6

TODAY'S SUNBEAM
YOUR GOOD MORNING NEWSPAPER

SERVING SALEM COUNTY, N.J., SINCE 1919, SUNDAY, JUNE 23, 1991

Local chef served famous U.S. generals

By MARY JANE THOMPSON
Staff Writer

WOODSTOWN -- Lorenzo M. Roberto approaches cooking with the same gusto that carried Gen. George S. Patton through World War II.

Youth, 16, Critical Afte[r]
Lawrence Car Mishap

A 16-year-old Lawrence Township youth remains in critical condition in the intensive care unit of Helene Fuld Hospital with head wounds suffered in a Friday night auto accident.

Enrico Lieggi of 30 Rossa Avenue was taken to the hospital by the Lawrence Township First Aid Squad following the 10:15 p.m. accident which occurred on Princeton Pike at Texas Avenue.

Lawrence police say Lieggi was riding in the rear seat of an auto driven by Norris D.

Fischer, 18, of 35 Forrest Av[e]nue when it collided with [a] parked car in the northbou[nd] lane of Princeton Pike.

Neither Fischer nor anoth[er] passenger in the front se[at] were injured.

Fischer told police the ac[ci]dent took place when [he] swerved to avoid another c[ar] which had cut him off. T[he] owner of the parked sed[an] was listed as Alex R. Galins[?] of Princeton Pike.

Charges are pending agai[nst] Fischer in the accident whi[ch] is under the investigation [of] Patrolman Peter Harmon a[nd] Robert Cranstoun.

In Loving Memory
Ennio and Gina Lieggi

Dad, you left us on a Sunday morning, November 13, 2022. Mom followed 49 days later on Sunday, January 1, 2023.

You courted in Italy and Princeton, married in Princeton, lived in Princeton, worked in Princeton, and raised your family in Princeton.

Dad, you worked from 1947 to 2010 at all the best venues in Princeton, with the title *Chef!*

Now, a year later, you are missed by your children, your grandchildren, and great-grandchildren.

Rest in Peace. You are at peace together forever and ever in the firmament of Heaven.

Love,
Your fourth son,
Peter Felix John Lieggi

31

bon appétit

EDWARD & RACHEL
AUGUST 25, 2018

FIRST COURSE
CAESAR SALAD

MAIN COURSE
(Please Select One)

CHICKEN BALSAMIC
Marinated Chicken Breast topped with Fresh Mozzarella Cheese
& Roasted Red Peppers served with an Aged Balsamic Reduction

CHATEAU BRIAND
The Classic Sliced Filet of Beef Tenderloin Served
with a Port Wine Reduction

BRANZINO AQUA PAZZA
Branzino simmered with Roasted Cherry Tomatoes & Spinach
in a Olive Oil and Garlic Broth

VEGETARIAN~CHEF'S CHOICE

CHILDREN 12 and under ~ Chicken Fingers & Fries

#DESTINATIONDLABIK

THE WHITE HOUSE
WASHINGTON

January 31, 1991

Dear Mr. Lieggi:

Thank you for your thoughtful message. I was moved
by your comments about the actions we have taken, in
cooperation with our coalition partners, to liberate
Kuwait and to restore stability to the Persian Gulf
region.

Saddam Hussein has sickened the world by the launching
of indiscriminate attacks that have terrorized and
killed innocent people. His blatant disregard for
international conventions regarding the treatment of
noncombatants and prisoners of war only strengthens
our resolve.

Operation Desert Storm is working. We are making
progress toward the objectives set forth by the international community. While there may be setbacks and
obstacles along the way, one thing is certain: we will
stay the course, and we will succeed. I am grateful
that our courageous troops face this historic challenge
knowing that they have the support of millions of people
around the world. We are all tremendously proud of the
job they are doing.

I am heartened that so many Americans are joining
Barbara and me in praying for our brave service men
and women and for their families.

Best wishes.

Sincerely,

Ggy Bush

Mr. Peter F. J. Lieggi
234 West Upper Ferry Road
Trenton, New Jersey 08628

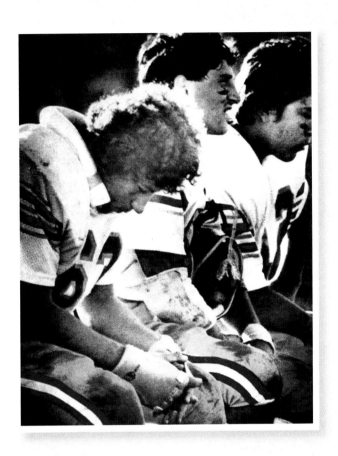

Deborah Dutch

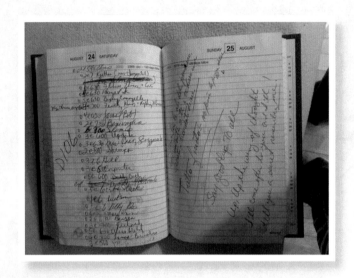

Scallopini of Veal Aristocratic for 2

For this recipe you will need 6 pieces of veal, 2 oz each and cut very thin, and flatten down three Slices of proscuitto cut in half, and 6 sliced fontina cheese or you can use mozzarella, with also 8 mushrooms cut into quarters, and 8 artichokes split in half. One teaspoon of chopped garlic , and a tablespoon of chopped parsley, with a ½ cup of flour, three tablespoons of oil, and 3 to 4 oz of white dry wine.

Have a sauté pan with two spoons of oil, and make hot. Pass the veal scallopini in The flour and cook for two minutes on each side, remove from the pan and drain off the excess oil, put the veal back in the pan cover with cheese and proscuitto. Meanwhile At the same time in a different pan with the other tablespoon of oil sauté the mushrooms, Artichokes, and garlic for 5 minutes. Put the mushrooms, and artichokes in the same pan with the veal. Make them hot and by adding the white wine and simmer it for 3 to 4 minutes. Sprinkle the chopped parsley and then serve. Enjoy.

Veal Chop or Costoletta di vitello ala Voldostana

For this dish you will need a veal chop from Natural Veal 1 inch thick, along with one slice of proscuitto di parma, 2 slices of Italian fontina cheese, and 3 spoons of oil or vegaetable oil. Two whole eggs whipped, with a spoon of chopped parsley. Salt and pepper and ½ juice from a lemon, and 4 oz of white wine, a teaspoon of balsamic vinegar, and 1 cup of flour.

With a boning knife make a 1 inch slit in the back of the veal chop and try to make a pouch without cutting the side. Roll the fontina cheese and proscuitto and place in the pouch of the veal. Mix the chopped parsley with the eggs. In a sauce pan add the oil and make moderate hot. Pass the veal chop through the flour , and dip it into the eggs and put it into the pan. Make the veal chop golden brown on both sides. Remove it from the fire and disgard any excess oil. Sprinkle with salt and pepper , balsamic vinegar, and the lemon juice. Then bake in the the oven at 375 degrees for 20 minutes, with it in the olive keep putting the white wine on it. Remove from the oven and from the pan onto a plate garnish it with parsley and serve.

Mr. Lieggi,

Unfortunately I am not able to get these cards signed for you. I really appreciated reading your letter. Thanks for writing. Go Sox!

From,

The Boston Red Sox

BONNIE WATSON COLEMAN
12TH DISTRICT, NEW JERSEY

HOUSE COMMITTEE ON
APPROPRIATIONS

HOUSE COMMITTEE ON
HOMELAND SECURITY

Congress of the United States
House of Representatives
Washington, DC 20515–3012

2442 RAYBURN HOUSE OFFICE BUILDING
WASHINGTON, DC 20515
(202) 225–5801

DISTRICT OFFICE:
850 BEAR TAVERN ROAD, SUITE 201
EWING, NEW JERSEY 08628
(609) 883–0026

WEBSITE: WATSONCOLEMAN.HOUSE.GOV

June 6, 2019

Mr. Peter F. Lieggi
30 Rossa Avenue
Lawrenceville, NJ 08648-3535

Dear Mr. Lieggi,

I am writing to you today because I would like to provide you an update you on the activities of the 116th Congress. My records show that you may be interested in government and voting reform, and so I would like to tell you about the *For the People Act* (H.R. 1).

On March 8th, 2019, the House of Representatives passed 234 - 193 H.R. 1, *For the People Act*. This important legislation, originally introduced by Rep. John Sarbanes (MD-3), ensures clean and fair elections, makes it easier for Americans to exercise their right to vote, reforms campaign finance systems, and puts in place national redistricting reform. H.R. 1 ensures that our elections belong to the American people.

I am proud to vote for legislation that puts democracy back into the hands of the American people. As a co-sponsor, I joined 236 of my colleagues to demand that Congress address issues in our election system. It is my priority to ensure that Congress serves the American people, and I am committed to restoring the people's faith in our government. As your representative, I will continue to fight for legislation that protects our democracy.

I hope that you find this update valuable, and I encourage you to continue to express your concerns and opinions with me and my office. As your representative, I value your input and participation in our democratic process. You can learn more about my activities in Congress by visiting my website at www.watsoncoleman.house.gov, contacting my office at 202-225-5801, and following me on social media. Again, thank you for expressing your thoughts to me.

Sincerely,

Bonnie Watson Coleman
Member of Congress

Dear Gina and Ennio
May you recall
with joy, today,
The special things
you've done
And lovingly reflect upon
Your memories, one by one...

God blessed you
in the kindest way,
And here's a little prayer
That God will keep
on bringing you
More happiness to share.

*I will celebrate Mass for
you and your intentions as
the best way I know of
saying Happy Healthy and Holy
Golden Anniversary
In Christ's Love, Fr. Toomer*

Happy
Anniversary

MR.
Favorite Restaurant: ~~Mrs.~~ Leiggi's Ewing
Manor. ("Oh, that chicken spezzatini!")

Favorite Fashion Designer: Halston. ("And
I wish I could afford him!")

Favorite TV Program: Masterpiece Theatre.

Favorite Vacation Spot: Anywhere in the
South of France.

Favorite Memory: "When our two children
were little, Ferd and I waited seven years
for them and then they came, twenty months
apart. What a joy to watch them grow!"

Favorite Pastime: Reading. ("I have four
books going right now.")

Favorite Newspaper: "It's The Trentonian,
mostly because it's a good community
newspaper, because it succeeds in being part
of our community. It's truly oriented to this
area.

---

*To Peter (1979)
with fond memories
Vin Josti*

Dedication

To Jerry — the young man in the red-and-gray tiger
sweater who greeted me each morning at my locker at NYU
with a single stem rose grown in his postage stamp-sized front
garden and kept fresh in a water-filled burette from the
chemistry lab, as well as to our beloved daughters, Kathy and
Debbie, and our cherished grandchildren, Jacob, Margaret,
and William.

New terrace on river

OPEN FOR BUSINESS — Banquet manager Joe Lieggi (left) and Josephine's restaurant manager Juan Rios discuss the location of tables at the Terrace Grill, which opened for business Friday at the Excelsior Hotel in Little Rock.

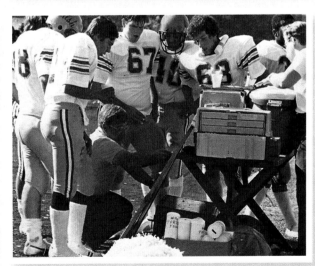

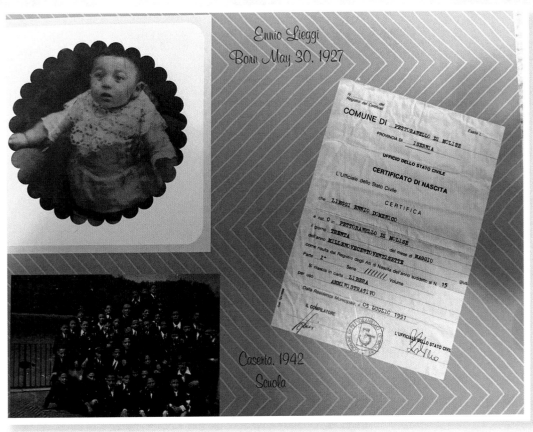

Ennio Lieggi
Born May 30, 1927

Caserta, 1942
Scuola

Italia 1947

1947   1947

53

1948

marzo 21- 1948

Married July 31, 1948

1948

1948

1948

First Love

A Gina

"Sono e sarò sempre il tuo Ennio"

Benvenuto in America

Linden Lane
1948-1951

New Years 1950

And Joe made three...

And JR made four...

Witherspoon Street
1951-1953

New Years 1952

Forrest Ave
1953-1958

And Paul made five...

And Peter and Timmy made six and seven...

The Scalini, Rome

Pettoranello

Orvieto

And the family keeps growing...

Rossa Ave
1958 to present

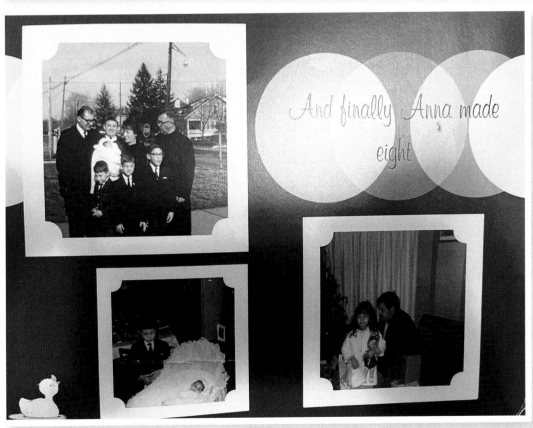

And finally Anna made eight

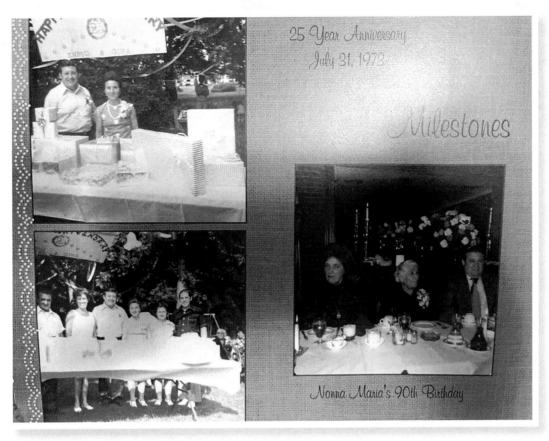

25 Year Anniversary
July 31, 1973

Milestones

Nonna Maria's 90th Birthday

50th Anniversary

80th Birthday

Always ready for a trip back to Italy...

Jesolo

Venice

Pettoranello

Pretty good...not bad for an old man...

CHAPTER 5

Having Kids and Earning a Living—1952-1976

As they evolved in marriage, Mom and Dad lived with Dad's folks for a while. When they moved out, they got an apartment on 287 Witherspoon and Nassau Street—exactly where, on Nassau Street I don't know, but they said it was good enough until they could afford their first house. It just would not be in Princeton, Dad was short and was too proud to ask his parents for funds. Dad and Mom gave And saved for his retirement was spent on his kids, and I am talking six figures.

Mom made sure while Dad worked, and on occasion played soccer on a Sunday, catholic doctrine was involved in our upbringing. Joe and Ennio Jr. were baptized, went to catholic school in Princeton, and learned Italian until a nun told Mom to try to speak English at home so they could learn the American way of life. Joe was the leader of his brother, and Junior idolized him. Soon, in 1953, Ennio and Gina bought their first of two homes in Lawrence Township, on 32 Forrest Avenue. They adapted well, as Ennio went to work and Gina kept house and handled the money. The deliveries of milk and bread came, and mom adapted as an American housewife. The delivery men's only question to Mom was, "Who's winning the World Series?" All housewives watched the afternoon games during the fifties.

They went to both churches, Saint Ann's and Saint Paul's, which were close for her and for his mother-in-law. They were like me: family men. They valued family and were all close, by except Felix in Trenton, and family comes first. It was convenient; around the corner, both Joe and Junior went to Saint Paul's all eight years. The new house on Rossa Avenue was built by Chester Rossa, and Mom paid a hundred-dollar deposit for it. With the help of Charles Draine, everything became possible. In 1957, Paul was born, and the new house was essentially bought by Mom because she hustled and negotiated with the builder on her own. The house was originally for him and his wife, but the flagship houses on the block, as usual, went to us! Money talks! They met their neighbors, the Feehans, on the left; Mom's brother lived on the right—now that's cozy! In 1961, on February 27, I was born.

Aunt Joan tragically passed in a car crash. Three others in the car that survived, as well as the driver from Vineland, and it changed life as they knew it. You see, it was the second death of a close family member, the first being Dad's brother in 1959. He Is buried in Our Lady of Lourdes not far from Saint Mary's. He was supposed to be buried in Saint Gregory's Church in Nottingham, but the priest at the time couldn't allow it, based on the fact he was married on a military base. That upset Dad so much that he refused to go to church. It was Monsignor Frain, at urging of Mom, who got him to go to church again. It ended over twenty years of grief for Dad, after the death met the front page of the Trenton Times newspaper in October of 1959. Then, they lost Mom's sister-in-law, her younger brother's wife. I really don't recall her but through pictures.

Life went on. We had a normal childhood, parties, and picnics. We all got together before the births of Glendale Inn and Lieggi's Ewing Manor. Glendale was the start and the pinnacle of ownership. It was a majestic restaurant on New Hillcrest and was one of the jewels of Ewing Township until we bought our own. It had more than four dining rooms, plus an adjacent apartment, and it was a place I enjoyed from 1972 to 1974. I played with the dishwashing machine at age eleven and got eggs made by cooks Gene Sanchez and Domingo. The waitresses were Dad's number one liaisons to serve his cuisine, while Uncle Tony and Domenic Tamasi manned the front. Mom took care of her house. Her mom was suffering from lung cancer, so she had three kids to raise and parents to tend to. Nonna Jenny passed on February 22, 1973, before my birthday, so it was a very sad birthday. I was the altar boy for the funeral ordered by Mom at Saint Paul's Church in Princeton. I cried my eyes out in the cemetery as the priest who conducted the mass in Italian held onto me; no one cared but Mom. We played baseball, and the game of life—and we didn't spit on someone's screen window like someone did once. Uncle Joe was a good uncle, as Tim lived with us, and soon Princeton football and basketball was a daily bus ride. The chaperone was Uncle Joe; as a youth, he adapted to the Princeton way of life. Tim moved in when his mother passed in 1962, our downstairs playroom was used until Uncle Joe remarried Aunt Wilma and their new house was bought in 1968.

Anna was born in 1966. Dad and Mom had their daughter, and their favorite. All of us went to Notre Dame High from 1963 to 1984; catholic doctrine was in force, and it was a good style introduced to us, whether we accepted it or not. Meanwhile, Dad went on to work daily at various restaurants. From Don Young's to Rickshaw in Cherry Hill, it was an adventure in seeing how one man could cook! After that, it did not matter how many times he left Don Young's, he always was asked back; he was considered the best not only by the help but also by the boss. Until Don Young's sold in the 1970 to Colonial Cadillac, Dad was the executive chef everywhere he went. He and his brother, Anthony, along with Domenic Tamasi, purchased Glendale Inn from Carolyn Hankin. Dad stayed until 1974, and then he went on to different places like Buckley's Tavern and Golden Goose while his kids evolved as young adults.

Family was essential. Even when Joe joined the US Air Force and Junior joined the Marines, they went on. Joe wrote daily, first stationed in Lackland Air Force Base, then Indianapolis, and finally, where he met the love of his life, Patricia Cartwright Williams. In 1973, we all met her at a wedding anniversary celebration at my uncle's home, which was a surprise to everyone but Dad, who stumbled on the surprise by accident. Ennio Jr. went to basic training but was honorably discharged due to the car accident when he was sixteen; he could not recoil the second shot on the firing range. To everyone's surprise, he came home, but Nonna Jennie was surprised the most.

Mom was confident enough in her driving ability to go back and forth to Princeton to see her mom and dad, and it made Mom happy. The letters from my godmother, Ann Toto Pagliaro—the patina, as we called her—were essential in her recovery from breast cancer. Ann was the epitome of godmother to five children, saving money for them in bank books; every Christmas, Easter, or birthday, she made it her business that her godchildren were protected from harm. Family is essential, would you not agree? She sent my notorious picture of the agony of defeat in football in 1978. Mom made it her business to see me play in November 1978, against Lawrence, and I was totally shocked when her name was announced. Neither ever came to see me play; they always listened on the radio to hear my condition, and especially when I was injured with a busted shoulder, concussion, or bruised ribs, they made me cry, and there was no crying in football in public.

I cried in private, because we lost the championship game and my girlfriend showed up. I don't know why. We were dating; she was the Mrs. Lieggi full-time in my life from September to November 1978. I kept it secret. She looked at me and I kept my eyes on her, crying inside as we were destroyed 24–0. I regret breaking up with her, but she found someone better than me. We came from two different worlds. I was used to never being loved—not from my parents, not from family. It was my prom date who taught me love, and Mom approved of her, but the girls from school couldn't handle her. My two female friends, two sisters in Christ, were my closest friends from 1978 to 1979 when we graduated. We went to movies and parties, Mom and Dad approved of them, and the two of them cared about me. I let them do everything and anything, like seeing the eyes of Laura Mars and letting them dig their nails in my arms. In 1977, I was invited to a party at a classmate's house in Ewing, on a Saturday. My cousin Tim dropped me off. It was when the Dodgers beat the Phillies, and a girl poured a beer over my head because she knew I like the Dodgers. It was when a girl and I bonded as she put a cigarette out in my palm for drinking like fish. She knew I'd thrown up on her rug. Back to the football game.

My Aunt Wilma was instrumental in making sure Mom attended the game, and the Class Moderator made sure she came. Mom came with Anna, and my cousins. It was homecoming and I was not nominated. It's not fair; it's like when no family comes to see you play. They are there to give you support whether you play or not, be victorious, and come back to earth knowing that you are human, just special for a while. Another incident, on June 25, 1978, was my first car accident, during which Mom and Dad really showed concern for their fourth son, when I cracked up the 1972 Chevy Nova of J.R.'s and almost passed away. I had entered the intersection where Pennington met Olden; she went through the red light and we collided. The car was totaled, and I was taken by ambulance to Mercer Hospital's emergency room for precautionary concussion protocol. Mom entered with Anna and was relieved I was alive, as they recalled J.R.'s accident

In 1967. Dad had entered the intersection sometime after the collision and was told he had nine lives. Dad and Mom catered to us before and after the restaurant was bought. We were all told of current events; Mom kept newspapers like the bicentennial in 1976, the death of John Paul II, and the papers of 9/11; and we listened to Dad's music and comedy album of Pat Cooper on the stereo record player. Dad loved watching television, especially war movies and all the shows of the era. Dad listened to Sinatra, Dean Martin, and Pavarotti, who he saw perform along with Sinatra thanks to Paul. Anyone who says differently didn't really know Dad. As for rock music, he tolerated it because we listened to it. He didn't go to a baseball stadium until Chicago in 2000 with Mom, Paul, Daniela, and me. It was the Cubs versus Padres, and the fact Phil Nevin of the Padres hit a home run was special to Mom because she'd never seen one before. Many things they experienced thanks to Paul and Joe, like Hot Springs, Arkansas, and in 2003, San Francisco, where I felt at ease while going to the waterfront and on trolley cars, and Mary Ellen was there too. We saw the Phillies beat the Giants, Pat Burrell, hitting the game winner.

Marriages took place, beginning with Joe in 1973. We traveled to Little Rock, Arkansas, via Washington DC, and a connecting flight from Philadelphia. We had no tube from the plane to terminal; we had to walk down. We were Yankees in Dixie. We had met Patricia in July of 1973 but did not know the particulars of his proposal. They met in the noncommissioned USO place, he proposed, and she accepted. She just said to herself that, by the way he carried himself, she knew he was the guy for her. They were wed in a Baptist ceremony; she was a Cartwright, and her maid of honor was her bestfriend, J.R. was best man, and the South got introduced to me. I pulled Paul's chair from under him to get back at him for chipping my tooth with his slingshot. I was a precious twelve-year-old getting over Nonna Jennie's death in February before my birthday that year.

In 1976, Ennio Jr. was married in a Catholic church in Bordentown, New Jersey, with two receptions: one at a VFW hall and the other at Mom and Dad's home, complete with buffet. Let's just say Ennio Jr.'s wedding to Ann Marie Matthews was special, but the outcome was that Michelle Lynn was born in October 1976, and the divorce came some four years later. Such is life. Paul was married by a celebrated judge of the court in 1986, and the reception and ceremony were held in the Westin Hotel. Anna married twice, once December 28, 1985, to Mark Eggert, God rest his soul. I liked him then. The ceremony was the first at the New Church of Saint Ann's in Lawrence by Monsignor Thomas J. Frain that involved two different religions—Mark was Presbyterian and Anna Catholic. There were three limos, a reception at a Marriott Hotel that doesn't exist anymore, and I took an employee as my date. Anna's second marriage was in 2002, six years after Alex was born, to George at a Presbyterian church in Pennington, New Jersey, with a reception over at my cousin's house. We all blew bubbles after the ceremony, Rachel and Alex's favorite thing to do. Also in 1985, Patricia sent a letter addressed to Captain Frank Reed, WNBC radio's all-request radio show, asking them to call Dad for his anniversary, which they did. The writer of the letter was me and dictated Patricia ask them to play either Billy Joel's "The Longest Time" or Frank Sinatra's rendition of the Paul Anka song "My Way." Dad chose "My Way."

The realm of doing nutty things started when they gave me a title, a good movie, called "You Never Said You Loved Me" for the family and me, as vice president followed and then general manager. The first title was treasury officer, like one of the Untouchables. In their generosity to the five children, they gave money to Joe to buy his house on Eggert's Crossing Road, as did I. Dad gave J.R. money to buy his house in Fallingston. Dad bought Anna a townhouse she paid rent at, and then we sold it, he gave her money to buy a home on Cleardale Avenue in Ewing, which they sold when George died. All Italian families wish is their offspring to be fruitful; we were not, except Anna with her two girls. The boys gave no sons to carry on the name. I am not counted out yet—the thing still works, I just need the right girl.

What I gave mom and dad was grief. In 1986, I learned, thanks to friends, how to snort cocaine, shoot speed, inject heroin, smoke hashish and weed, and be cross-addicted. It started In February innocently, and it just got worse. I learned how to hide it and lie to Mom and Dad as well as myself. The ninety-dollar-a-week addiction that was literally killing me was actually myself. I looked for drugs at the restaurant. They never suspected a thing. A gram and a half of speed, a gram of coke, a spoon of heroin, and I was very happy lying to get the needles. I stayed out late with a friend, may he rest in peace. A friend called me drug addict after a deceased basketball player. My friends from Saint Anthony's cared. I partied at Rutgers, Rider, and TSC, and I was on the late-night radio on TSR with a classmate who is a DJ, Notre Dame Class of 1979. I went to Sea Isle City to come down. It was there that I opened up to a roommate whose last name I didn't even know.

I was afraid of love, even from her, always wondering if Mom and Dad would approve of her. She was a blonde, my type. When we met, she said, "I have heard so much about you!" Not knowing exactly what she'd heard, I was flattered, thinking that this could be something, but alas, so drunk, I went straight to sleep, thinking of her. The trick was not to get on anyone's bad side by grabbing someone I didn't know. When I went to Fort Lauderdale to see a friend, I didn't care about my girlfriend anymore, but the hurt was huge in December of 1986, and I used the connections of the business to arrange my trip. Totally hitting bottom for five days, as the drugs were totally out of my system, and thinking of my mortality, I ran wild, going from girl to girl. Mom and Dad worked, and if they suspected anything, it was a great white lie and secret to me; my family was oblivious to the addiction. Losing tremendous amounts of weight and losing my other girlfriend was too much for me to bear.

Princeton House couldn't stop an addiction in 1987, but Carrier finished the job in 1994. It depends on how much denial is in you. I totally broke down while watching a movie called "You Never said You Loved Me", uncontrollably crying like a child, because of the PTSD I had from traumatic experience in Chicago and New Jersey. The thing was, we had cocaine even there. It was a battle to stay clean. Two weeks in rehab was enough for me, as I was in denial, but I still won a hundred dollars curtesy of the Giants beating the Broncos. Mom and Dad weren't able to understand that the youngest son was being destroyed by the guilt of letting them down and his friends, who themselves were in denial, especially when they accused him of leading them into a life of addiction. Mom and Dad didn't know the Pandora's Box that had been opened in 1987. When going to Florida to get a girl, Mom asked a friend, "Is this necessary?"

The thing is, business suffered. We were in debt because of a bad accountant advice, two real estate agents were hired to sell the place. Dad was fed up. It's all my fault; it's all my fault. The thing is, the selling stopped in 1988; we went off with no sale. Others tried to entice us to leave; no one had the money upfront. We don't have mortgages like others. You hold a mortgage and you can lose it all. It was a battle to stay clean, hiding from Dad. Mom wasn't stupid, always changing my hiding places, not only at home but also at the restaurant. To be honest, did I want death? Maybe! Why else would I shoot up and drink myself to death? From the time a girlfriend dumped me, for no good reason, I was on a bad path. The restaurant was the fuel to what I needed—getting a beer for Dad and a beer for me. The more money I made, the more I wanted that white powder or liquid speed. I had plenty of spoons I used and tossed into the garbage, booze, food to eat at past midnight, and places to cry inside the restaurant. Two new friends, and the madness in 1994 was gone. Rachel was born.

One funny story about how Rachel is the favorite is that, when she was born, we showed her off in the dining room like she was the crown princess of the restaurant. She was the best event of the winter of 1994. Her birth was also the last rehab for cocaine addiction that had started in December of 1993. I was in Carrier Clinic, lying my ass off to conceal addiction until my mom found out who ratted me out. Two weeks was all I needed. Plus, I was at Rider University, trying to get a degree no one approved of. Two weeks went by, and I was back in classes, and three years later, I earned my bachelor of science in business administration. It was an achievement that no one could deny. Even the Patron loved it, and he loved that children were back in my life. So was my family, as one time she got her little finger caught in the door—a simple cut, but it lasted a lifetime for the little peanut as it was. That pissed off Mom at Dad and me, and then Anna yelled at Mom for yelling at me, and a Patron from the bar could be heard suggesting, "Give her some ice cream; that will work!" It worked.

Rachel and Alex were babysat constantly by me, and I let them do anything while I did the bookkeeping on Saturdays. One time, Rachel and Alex went up the second floor to play hide and seek. All of a sudden, Rachel came running from the dining room, sat down, and said her butt hurt. I thought nothing of it until Alex came in and proudly said, "Uncle Pete, Rachel fell through the ceiling!"

Startled, I went out to the dining room and saw how she fell through a ceiling tile from the old stairway, which had been boarded up by Mary Marks. I simply asked if she was okay. As she nodded her head, and George and Dad laughed, I said, "Mom will not be laughing! Neither will Anna." So, we got a ceiling tile from the kitchen, replaced it, swept and vacuumed the debris, and thought nothing of it. Mom was no idiot. She noticed the missing tile, and we told her it was the rain.

The first words out of her mouth when she went to the ladies' room were, "Liar! Who did what?" We had told her it was the rain; it hadn't rained—lie one. Then, when we told her the truth, all she did was shake her head and say, "God Bless America!"

That is why the true gift to our family was girls, though which ones depends on themselves. Offspring was essentially the grace of God, as first Michelle Lynn was born in Helene Fuld Hospital in Trenton in 1976, joining step-granddaughter Kimberly, followed by Daniela Elizabeth in Chicago in 1989, and then Rachel Lynn in Mercer Hospital in Trenton in 1994, and finally, the favorite Alexandra Marie in 1996 at the same hospital. The best thing was that Dad and Mom got to live, go to the wedding, and see one granddaughter marry. Rachel was wed on August 25, 2018, at the Merion Caterer of Cinnaminson, complete with bridesmaids, ushers, and best man, in a excellent ceremony. Eddie proposed to Rachel on Christmas Eve in 2016, in front of my parents, in their house, in the living room, and with their blessing. Rachel said yes, and my dad walked her down the aisle like the grandfather he was, to the outside venue at the Merion with two-hundred-plus guests. He famously said, "Bon Appetite," as he did so many times at the dining room table. They paid for their wedding with a little help—a little from me and a little from Dad—but the rest they paid in full on their own.

The reason the father of the bride didn't pay was that, five years before, he had passed away. George was a family man with Sunday family day, and the brain cancer that claimed him would alter his family's destiny. The glue was gone, and bad choices were inevitable without that man to be an obstacle. He passed on a Monday; I didn't find out till a text message at work alerted me. My babies were in tears, and I wasn't there to console them. My anger at Mom and Dad that night was fierce. No job is more important than a child who needs a father figure to reassure them. To be blind is one thing, but to be uncaring doesn't work with Peter Felix John Lieggi. The funeral was somber; the soccer team showed up like they had done at the benefit. My niece's friends were there, and my fellow three Knights of Columbus, Council 7000, were there for emotional support for me. A motorcycle escort to the grave I donated in Ewing Cemetery was the end of that chapter. Since then, Alex finally gave birth to Darryl George in 2017, in a hospital in Tampa, Florida, where she could deliver without drama. Rachel gave birth to Madison Grace—or Maddie, as we call her—in 2020, during the pandemic, while I was working at FedEx Ground in Hamilton; she gave birth to Riley in 2023. Mom never got to see her third great-grandchild in the flesh, but saw her, but like Maddie, she did see the ultrasound in Capital Health Hopewell before her birth.

CHAPTER 6

Owning Lieggi's Ewing Manor
Restaurant—1976-2002

The restaurant Mom and Dad are most known for was bought in the fall of 1976, with the help of Armando Conti of Trenton Beverage Company. They secured the loan by Robert Cerny: a modest $250,000, payable in ten years at a modest $1,000 and change a month, with $175,000 going to Mary Marks, the proprietor of Mary Marks Ewing Manor. The sale almost didn't happen, because Mom had stage four breast cancer. The doctors at Princeton Medical Group were reluctant to operate, so it was decided after much discussion—as they told mom—that she would not last until December of 1976. At that time, she was to go to Memorial Sloan Kettering Hospital in New York City and be operated on by Dr. Urban, who also operated on a Rockefeller. So, in September of 1976, Mom had a mastectomy; the cancer was gone, her boob was gone, and she was cancer-free and would remained so for forty-seven years, until she passed away on January 1, 2023.

Anna and I were not told. All we were told was that Mommy was sick, and she had to go to New York. We found out after the surgery. If I had known my mother was dying of cancer, I probably would not have played varsity football as a sophomore. I got into a fight with a teammate after he called her a slut, and like Mr. Spock, I could not control my anger because my mother meant more to me than life itself. Anna, on the other hand, was always asking, "Why is Mommy crying?" We found out the night before Dad and Mom went to New York, while dad was working at the Golden Goose in Hamilton, as he paid a chef friend to work for him. She came into the bedrooms and kissed us each on the forehead as if to say, "It was nice knowing you." Dad did the same thing on January 12, 1999, before his bypass surgery for his ailing heart. It was anger and his shame in leaving saying, "I am leaving, but the fight still remains," and he won. We drove up to New York for Mom's operation, as I got off from football practice. In the words of my head coach, it was a legitimate excuse. I saw my mom, and in tears, I went down and got a hot dog and came back. It seems as if, every time there's an operation, like there was with Dad, either a New York hot at a dog or a Philadelphia hot dog is involved. All we wanted to do was take her home where she belonged—to her home in Lawrence Township, where her taxes were being paid and the restaurant had then become reality.

The one thing that most restaurants don't do is experience Front Street in Philadelphia. Dad and I would drive down, if not in the van we bought from Elvira and Bob Singer, then the station wagon or SUV to purchase produce and fish from the best suppliers off the dock, such as Leone, Eckert, or Kallish. We got seafood from Blue Crab Seafood, who succeeded Century Seafood, and the man who took the checks or from cash-only Bert. We would drive from 4:30 a.m. to reach the market at 5:15 on a Wednesday and, with cash, buy what we could save from local purveyors. Drivetime radio was Don Imus or WMMR, depending on who was driving. Dad drove down and I drove back, and it was a great experience of father-son time and business learning. That is what makes a five-star restaurant, and no one can deny that. We took a dolly and our muscle to bring back what was essential: iceberg lettuce, romaine, tomatoes, mushrooms, lemons, and odds and ends. As for fish, it was Norwegian salmon, live lobster, yellowtail or flounder, bulk crabmeat, scrod, softshell crabs, shad and shad roe, clams, oysters, and the ever-popular lobster tail for surf and turf.

Our creditors were the key. We started with three butchers, predominantly the best money could buy: Caesar Meats, led by the Donini Brothers of South Clinton and Hamilton Avenues; Dutch Meats of Ewing; and City Beef on Willow Street in Trenton. Extra desserts were once Joan Specter's Chocolate Moose and Michelle Lorie Cheesecakes on Hamilton Avenue or Landolfi's, whose rum cakes were made with real rum. Seafood was an adventure, as Marsh's Crab Trap, Atlantic seafood, would be rivaled by Century Seafood, Blue Crab Seafood, and the very local P and G Trading Company of Ott Street, Trenton. Ice cream was buy-two, and they were best, especially Ralph Goldstein's R and R Ice Cream, who brought tartufo, tiramisu, spumoni and tortoni, and flavored ice cream in a shell; and Arctic Ice Cream of Arctic Parkway in Ewing. We bought produce from the famous Licciardello Family, International Produce, Blue Eagle, and Luca Mushrooms. Our milk men were the ever-popular Rosenberger Dairies of Pennsylvania, and Saxony Ice Company of Trenton when the ice maker would break down, until Mike of L and M refrigeration would repair it.

Don Walker's Miller Mobil was our mechanic, followed by his protégé who plowed the snow in Ewing off Wilburtha. Edward Don was our supplier for silverware and dishes, followed by Singer Equipment Company, White House Chemical, and Crystal Chemical Company, and John Hunsberger was salesman and servicer of the dishwasher. Our electrician was George Prince of Lambertville, followed by his protégé Carl Darby. The best waste disposal was handled by John Zuccarelli, who gave Dad a break because business was not good in the beginning and we almost folded. Mom didn't know the word "quit" by anyone. We got a little satisfaction when Armando Conti said, "My name is Conti. You are not quitting." He provided free service for six months in the beginning to get Dad on his feet. His waste management company was the best. They didn't know how to give up, and neither did we; thanks to men like John Zuccarelli, we made It. He brought the great Jake LaMotta one day with Joey Giardello.

Our other purveyors included Latona Foods of Carlstadt, New Jersey; Gardner Good Foods of Trenton; Trenton Frozen Foods; Sexton; Kraft Rosenblum; and Alessio

Import Products, who serviced and delivered expresso. Liquor companies included Tony Sparano's Capitol Wine and Liquors, Joe Berger with Allied Beverage, George Massisin with J and J Distributing Company, and Skip Hutchinson's Royal Liquors. Beer distributors were the Ryan-Natale Ritchie and Page Distributors, and salesman Rich Arbitell of Hub City Distributors. For fires, we had JW Kennedy and Sons and United Steamway Systems taking Care of the screens. Linen was by Sanitary Linen, Garden State Linen, and Gemini Linen. Fuel for heating was Nassau Oil or Tattersall and Princeton Fuel. Our clientele was made of professional businesspeople. A lot I could name, like Ron Rick of Rick Bus Company and his brother T.R. of TR's Tire in Ewing. For A couple weeks, his brother Buddy worked as well. I don't forget good workers like him.

Like Leo Smolar of the local McDonald's franchises, Dr. Thomas Bills, and his parents. Like the owners of Reedman Car Dealership, who Dad bought two cars from; every Saturday, without fail, they were there. Like fine wine, they aged gracefully. There was the Kelly Family, Rita Mae Thomas and the Flahives; their farewell letters are still with me. Francine and Michael Kjettsa had Dad autograph a menu on the last day. Mrs. G and her granddaughter Debbie would bring the twins. Herb Gross and Mr. Silverstein of Trenton Stove and Repair; car dealership owners, on occasion; Don Young and Don Ottaunick; Dad's former bosses, and Joe Samerone of Golden Goose in Hamilton were all good men. From men like Judge Richard J. S. Barlow Jr. to Mary Roebling, with her granddaughters and her daughter Betty Hobin, especially her actress granddaughter Debbie Dutch of Hollywood, California; porcelain maker Helen Boehm to the legendary Kirov Ballet of Leningrad, USSR, they were exceptional.

It was June 1986, and Mom and Dad agreed to cater to the Mercer County Chamber of Commerce and Shelly Zeiger and welcome the ballet troupe. Perestroika was the order of the year and, thanks to Dutch's tenderloins, Licciardello's beans and potatoes, and Latona's pasta, Ed Meara poured the cold cases of champagne. They brought dignitaries galore of Mercer County, notably the Mercer executive Bill Matthius, assemblyman John Watson, and Carmen Armenti of Trenton, to my Walkin box. I never saw a member of the KGB until that day, and I remember what the kitchen was like. The blinds were closed, the second floor guarded, and security galore. They came, they ate, they autographed, they enjoyed, and they left. I think Mom made Pravda, and I know she made the Times of Trenton. Mom was happy and so were Helen Gazda and Dana Stannard, their servers. The rest I didn't see, but it was an honor to serve those who enjoyed Dad's food of the day! My mom would always visit. It didn't matter whether it was Princeton House, Princeton Hospital, or Carrier—until she told Carrier, "I want my son home now; enough of this shit, I will handle it."

Once, we had a military wedding of two young soldiers who went in the Gulf War in 1991. We had many anniversary parties and rehearsal dinners, engagements, and good first-time dates for couples during the ever-popular Valentine's Day dinners. The parties by Walter Kavanaugh kept us afloat, as he would pay by check and include a little more that would carry over to future dinners or lunches. Thank God for the New Jersey legislature. Trenton

Country Club was the main club at the restaurant, with the best members on Fridays: Judges Daniel O'Donnell and Dave Schroth, Herb Moore, the Readings, and the Strattens.

The gang of undertakers—Henry Murphy, Peter Hodge, and Bob Wilson—were the best as well, though none were necessary to bury three pets. After my birthday in 1978, Dad found Blackie dead on the floor of the back room with Baron by his side. Dad called the vet, and they told him what to do after looking at him. He was buried near the tree line behind the restaurant without a marker. Baron was killed by a driver, an African American man who came in and told us he hit our dog. That night, Joe, Pat Quill, Mike Micinski, and I went down to check on Baron, who'd somehow broken the chain near the doghouse, before it was time to bring him in. Good guard dogs are hard to come by. Both were introduced to the family by J.R. Blackie was my dog, who we got as a puppy and who was always by my side.

My Blackie dying on my birthday was the last straw. I became indifferent to anyone else's suffering until Baron passed in 1984. It hurt so bad after the second car hit him, in the middle of the street in front of the driveway, near the sign. It is fitting he was buried by Dad and Cousin Gerry beside the shed, near a neighbor's side. The third was Anna's dog Damien, before Rachel and Alex were born, who was replaced by Othello. They had nowhere to bury him, because they lived in my parents' townhouse, which was an investment. Damien was buried behind the restaurant near tree line where Blackie was. Dad said okay because it was his daughter, who he could never say no to her.

There were the state troopers led by Johnny Aarms, Ross Bayer, and Major Spalding, as well as Lieutenant Genz, Captain Larry Larsen, Captain Jimmy Graham, and Captain Burns, to name a few. There were the union representatives Davey Jones, Kenny, and most notably, Tommy Isrycki, another honorary son of my mom's. He was a character and was the Polish prince of the NJSP, as a high school called him, and maybe he was right. I was there in the head, because girls played with it. Mom did not like any Local girls; they weren't fitting to have her son, who was so holy. We had people of the Jewish faith on Saturdays like Louis Linowitz, Leonard and Renee Punia, lawyers Joe Markowitz, Michael Zindler, Seymour Kaplan, and Natalie Marcus. Mom had her own favorite customers who were like friends, like Mary Clark with her affinity for Yankee baseball that Mom said was J.R.'s domain, since he won the bet against a patron during the 1978 Red Sox Boston Massacre: two hundred dollars. Yes!

We also had a regular named Governor Brendan Byrne, who would come in the kitchen to see my father and give him a pen, as if to say, "Write!" Chef's don't write, their sons do; that is why I write this. Then, there were leftovers from Mary Marks, whom we basically inherited, like her three nieces who were servers: Betsy, Iola, and Marie Mattonelli. Other employees were Mary Bonnani and Skurkie and Norman Edge. Our first staff was Joan Fallon, JoAnn Foss, Kathy Collins, and Sue Sharp, followed by Helen Gazdar. Always photograph your help; it shows who is true and who is fake. Kitchen help was a joystick of revolving doors. After Norman left, there was Evandos

Cheeseborough and Alfonso Earl, may they rest in peace. The part we didn't know was how Jairo Arzayus would turn out with his cousin Henry Zerna. That is for someone else to write. Bob McCall and Bill Nice were cooks.

Uncle Joe Ruberto who literally saved Dad's health in 1987 and was the reason Dad would have quadruple bypass surgery on January 12, 1999, and be out of action in an icy winter before the turn of the century. The last party dad worked before surgery was when the altar rosary was blessed by Josephine Gagliardi. A nine-hour operation at University of Pennsylvania in Philly scared Dad, and scared Mom, but two angels pulled him through, as Rachel happily announced in the kitchen, "We are going to see Nonno in the hospital." Nonno Joe took her. Dad told the story of climbing out of a ditch with those two angels saying, "Come on, Nonno!" In the words of a customer named Tom, Dad was in the zipper club, and it was like changing a tire. He came with Ed and Nancy Badgeley and Jim and Roianne Morford on Tuesdays and Thursdays.

We knew Dad had a bad heart because of our third trip to Italy. In 1982, Dad returned to his homeland after Mom said, "Enough is enough, let's go home." Thirty-five years after he left his town, we flew to Rome: Anna, Mom, Dad, and me. We stayed at the hotel Savoy near the American Embassy. During that two-week stay, we saw a lot: the Colosseum; the Vatican, with the big crowd that welcomed the first Polish-born Pope, John Paul II, during his weekly Wednesday audience in the courtyard outside the Vatican; Tivoli Gardens, tasting fine wine, which for Dad and Mom was heaven; trains to Firenze and Venice, meeting up with Luigi's nephew our guide to several towns, including a beach where girls didn't wear tops. I liked it! In Jesolo, we stayed not at a hotel but at his house. Then, on to Pettoranello by train, from Venice. It was a good train, better than the one from Firenze. The train to Dad's town was fun, and we met a couple from Chicago. They spent time talking to Anna, because she was sixteen years old and innocent then. Kids in their teens open up more to others who speak the same language in a foreign country.

In Dad's hometown, we met more cousins, especially Camilio Paoilino, the mayor of the town, and Cousin Gemma Nini's sister Maria and her spouse Mario Lombardozzo. Then, we went on to Carpinone, where a relative's son took Anna and me to Monte Cassino. The cemetery was enormous, and the memories my dad said were true. Whether members of my family fought there on both sides, only God knows. It was over eighty years ago; most are deceased and gone. Mom and Dad went again in 1988 with Joe and his wife Patricia to celebrate their fortieth wedding anniversary. Their fiftieth anniversary was publicized. We went again, this time with a grandchild. Dani came to her nonno and nonna's land to celebrate with them. From Firenze, to Positano, to Pettoranello, to Roma, we had a great time. Usually, I would go to a café to see what was out there, but if I decided to have fun, someone might get bent out of shape. This was when we found out Dad had blockage, in 1998, and it caused the bypass surgery that he had in 1999.

It was a necessary trip because he wished it, but 1987 was when I knew the restaurant was important. I had an episode in my apartment; smoking cigarettes damaged my lungs severely, to the point I had an asthma attack. Dad took me to Princeton. I laid on a gurney. I was so cold. I reached out for the nurse's hand to say, "Don't let go!" I died that day in October; what kept me here, I don't know. Maybe it wasn't my time yet to go. For a week, I was in a hospital room. No one came, so why I should care about others? It was reality to me: I was alone, thanks to them for showing me how fake they truly were. Family came; this was no rehab.

Anyway, back to our great customers. There was Tom McHale, Gene Urbaniak, and Dr. Sackswilner, as well as Ray Marks, the former owner, who came to dinner with his wife and family. There were the Barrets, the Bells, the Hughes Family, Joe McKee, and Jim Silimeo. We had the Naval Air Propulsion to Mercer County engineers and electricians, Ewing Kiwanis for parties, the Altar Rosary Society of Saint Ann's, and the priests of the Dioceses of Trenton to bless us. Monsignor Thomas N. Gervasio, of Saint Joachim–Saint Anthony's–OLS, loved his first parish of Saint Joachim. He was transferred by my friend and customer Reverend Monsignor William F. Fitzgerald of Our Lady of Good Council. We also had Father Harry E. Cenefeldt; Monsignor Thomas Frain; Monsignor Vincent Gartland of Saint Ann's; Bishops John M. Smith and John Reiss, may they rest in peace; Monsignor George Ardos of Saint George in Titusville; Monsignor Walter Nolan and Sister Dorothy Jancola; Monsignor Toomey, who dined with Helen Boehm of Boehm Porcelains; and Sister Mary Dismas of Notre Dame along with Sister Beth Dempsey of Saint Ann's, sisters of mercy. We were good. How can I forget Bill Faherty and Mayor Arthur Holland, who loved crabmeat au gratin for lunch, or David Hobin with his golden buck!

Every now and then, we had to take customers to court for nonpayment. Usually, it was conducted by John Cannon, esquire, to receive what we were due; it was usually house charges, involving patrons, and the rest. Sometimes, we ate it, when there were extenuating circumstances and they could not pay. The honor system of the house charge was the responsibility of Ennio Jr., Dad, and Mom for feeling sorry for them. They were hungry, they wanted the best, and they wanted a place to feel at home. Others took advantage because they went out of business, like someone who won't be named.. Advertising on radio and newspaper was by choice, especially the one by me during drive and lunch time on January 8, 1992, the fifteenth anniversary of the restaurant, and on WPST 97.5 FM by Nassau Broadcasting, for a decent nine hundred dollars per week. We tried advertising special nights Tuesday through Thursday and special meals, but they took advantage. They wanted It during the weekend, or if we were out of a dish like crabcakes, because they were made fresh, we were told we were doing false advertising on the menu.

We sold in 2002, because it was time to explore new things and new adventures. And put up with no more bullshit, Paulie Villereal forked over $475,000. Thanks to his attorney, Edward S. Kahn, Dad increased his investment by $300,000. We even had a press release scheduled but thought otherwise, a good move on our part. *Bona fortuna* to them. They lasted twelve years, not twenty-six like us, but at least they left with their shirt on. Mom and Dad never entered, even though they were invited.

CHAPTER 7

Life after Restaurant Ownership, and the Eventual End of the Road

Some eight years went by, as Dad officially, absolutely, retired in 2010, when he quit Nassau Inn. The state of New Jersey's department of labor refused to give him unemployment, and he had just cause. You see, Dad worked part-time, and the union didn't give a damn. It was one big set up the day I got laid off: July 20, 2010. We are not stupid, and we know when we are not wanted. Dad went to work part-time for the Nassau Club and five years for the Nassau Inn with me. For eight years, he swore he would never enter a bad place again, nor would Mom, who got bad lamb shanks once. Several years before, in December of 2007, Mom's appendix went sour, and she needed emergency surgery in Princeton Hospital on Witherspoon Street, where all her kids had been born. Like out of a movie, she came home before Christmas. Rachel and Alexandra visited her, and so did Dad and I after work at Notre Dame. Lori Rabon, our boss, was sympathetic, asking, "How's mom?" It was a very scary moment; also that year, I had my scare from my stress fracture in my left heel. I collected disability while being examined by both Dr. John Smith of Princeton Orthopedics and Dr. Thomas Bills of Mercer Bucks. Ironically, I returned to work on Thanksgiving on a limited basis, until I received the green light to return full time.

So, the year of 2007 was excellent, as was April 2005, when Mom and Dad witnessed their niece Linda's nuptials to Joel Hahn in Breckinridge, Colorado, with Anna. I could have gone, but I didn't know there are exceptions to the rule about no time off during hotel peak times. So, in all essence, Dad began working in Princeton in 1947 and ended in Princeton in 2010. Mom went to work in a bakery for the fun of it. Not long. In between, they had two consolations First was watching Rachel play soccer in Ewing travel, Ewing middle and high schools, and at Notre Dame from 2008 to 2010; she was junior varsity at Notre Dame her freshmen and sophomore years and varsity at Ewing her junior and senior years. One year, she played together with Alexandra. Then, the athlete went as a walk-on at MCCC, my alma mater, and she excelled. I would show mom and dad pictures and videos of their favorite grandchild, who also went to school to be a physical therapist. She couldn't finish, because her dad's passing in 2013 meant that anatomy was not her favorite subject. Alexandra went on to LIM, in New York City, and didn't finish after two years, but at least like Michelle, she made an attempt, as she did at Penn State. The graduate, excelled at Walter Payton High School and Loyola of Chicago University. She is gainfully employed, so the offspring have excelled one way or another, even through setbacks.

From 2017 to early 2023, their health suffered. Dad would put a pizza box in the oven to heat it, and I would object. Mom would say, "What is your problem?" When I would say it's not safe, I would be told to shut up. Offering wine to repairman was not kosher. They only once approved of a girl, who I brought home from a date at the restaurant when I opened up to her about what I did there when I was an addict. She cried for me. I cried too, in the dining room where I'd tried to shoot up in back in 1986, after hours, with a bottle of beer from the bar and the lights off. I missed. She turned down the offer, and on August 26, 2017, I was the only person setting up the tables in the ballroom. Mom said that day, "Do you want ring back? I have been holding." I said I wasn't sure she was the one. Girls I dated, like a girl turned me off because I did not need any more drama on headplaying. I was fifty-six and every single girl was hesitant. Why? Was it the history of infidelity or the fact that my mental health had been screwed up by poor choices. Did the girls know or care about the damage they did to me? No! There were phone calls of people saying nothing, at all hours of the day, for telling them it was the drug dealer or me. They chose their cross-addiction. I endured the rehabs I wanted to be drug free, in dad's words.

Dad was in the throes of dementia, but when it came to me, he was night and day. Best friend and worst enemy, every day. He had dementia and bad heart, plus he was ornery and stubborn like an old Italian. For three years, he was taken care of by his daughter and several others, and he suffered before succumbing on the Sunday morning of November 13, 2022. The stroke inflicted Mom, who had been put through enough. The house was occupied by family, and sometimes we would get on each other's nerves, but that is for another time and book. They died as they lived: with dignity. It was no surprise that Mom followed forty-nine days later, on January 1, 2023, in Greenwood House. We used family friend Frank Immordino and the Brenna Funeral Home on Klockner Road in Hamilton, New Jersey. Funerals followed at Saint Ann's, performed by Father Leandro "Lines" Dela Cruz and Deacon Gene Lanzoni with orchestration by Tom Carter and his beautiful cantor, Angela Marino, who sang a beautiful "Ave Maria." As family flew in and friends came, past and present, Dad and Mom were laid to rest in Saint Mary's, in Hamilton, New Jersey. Their love affair started in 1941 and ended in 2023 on this earth, but the next chapter is in the firmament of heaven.

CHAPTER 8

A Son's Point of View

Mom was sent with Dad to Arkansas in 2019. I wasn't qualified. They returned in October 2019. My sister gave up her career to care for them; I was the observer, watching mom, who was then paralyzed, and Dad, who had leukemia and dementia. It was not bad in the beginning, but soon, in 2020, the strokes hit. In 2021, the strokes were severe for Mom. All I had was a therapist to properly vent; while, at times, I did not like what I saw, only truly gifted people with medical training should be caregivers, and no doubt about that. I stayed up and worked during the early pandemic, until COVID-19 and a disability of the leg made manual work impossible.

Cleaning Dad's backside, watching the nurses clean Mom's backside, emptying refuse receptacles, being the verbal punching bag, cleaning mom, and being a mother to her own children at the same time, Anna did the best she could. Seven days a week, twenty-four days a day, she burdened herself with power of attorney over their affairs, always trial and error. She had no help from three brothers. Why, I don't know. Medicaid kicked in, hospice care, hospital beds, tension, tempers, getting vaccinated, and constant testing. There was mistrust from people who are uneducated in life and dealing with their own issues.

By then, Dad's dementia was totally in control of his mind, and he asked where the car was and where his restaurant was. He wanted to take the bus to Witherspoon street to pass away in the old hospital, which was not there anymore. He was crying for mama, defecating and urinating himself. It was a constant challenge to clean him up. Not even J.R. could handle It. In October, the eldest boys heeded their sister's cry to commit Mom and Dad to a nursing facility. Once they were admitted, she left immediately for Florida, leaving me alone to make sure both of them were well cared for. At times, he was given a drug to stifle him, and it made him sleep. Anger swept Dad, as he could not Believe what Anna had decided on his fate. I saw it, the nurses saw it, and the aides from Enoble saw it.

He passed first, and she cried, "Daddy died." His passing was empty and without last rites. Mom passed forty-nine days later, but this time, with glorified dignity. They watched mom better that time, because someone put up a stink, and it stuck that time. I was there like a pest to make sure she was well tended to twice a day, while Anna went to Florida. This is what a caregiver sees: neglect by no fault or intent. We said prayers, Glory Be's, Our Fathers, Hail Marys, and "Thou shalt walk into the valley of death alone." The grandkids and great-grandkids were there. She passed quietly, in one last gasp. The funeral was rushed, the eulogy by her, because the sons did not make an attempt to use their seniority. There were perfect sermons, the perfect cantor named Angela Adams, who sang like an angel for a woman who deserved Pavarotti: "Ave Maria" for her and "Time to Say Goodbye" for him.

No tears from me. The friends who never came, and the family who came and knew, were physically able. For those who didn't know, the state cared. The state they catered to had a sponsored proclamation from Senator Shirley Turner to honor Mom for twenty-six years at Lieggi's Ewing Manor in Ewing. The restaurant owner that took it upon himself to offer sympathy. Thank you, Steven Jordan and Blooming Grove Inn, for that and for the luncheon, and thanks to Marsilio's Kitchen down the street from the restaurant. That will be with me forever, until I can forgive myself for not using my wealth to care for them myself from 2017 to 2023.

The End of being a Caregiver

The End of an Era, as Named by Arnold Ropiek of the Trenton Times

This book is dedicated to the offspring of my brothers, my sister, my sister's girls, and my five nieces, who shine every day. For one grand-nephew, I have high hopes he will treasure everything his nonna and nonno did for him, from Alex giving birth to giving money for not just tuition, food, and clothing, but also an abundant home, a business that the old man didn't need, and those connections that got their kids ahead in life, both financially and with a job. Mom and Dad received nothing from their parents; all they did for us was from money given for their own homes and from their hearts. All they did they did for us, and they deserve to be remembered in both good works and song. The old man worked five, six, sometimes seven days a week, making peanuts for a wage. His wife took his check and saved for three houses from 1953 to 2023. None can doubt their righteousness and what they did for ninety-five and ninety-four years of life; role models for Catholics around the area, and locally loved by their neighbors, how can that be captured in an epitaph?

They professed their vows, "Till death we do part!" Mom made sure to keep the sabbath holy by taking her children to church every Sunday. They both honored thy father and thy mother. Every holiday, especially Catholic holidays, they lived their faith. They donated extensively to the Church of Saint Ann, not once, twice, or thrice, but many times. Their names are on the boards of dedication in the school, church, faith development center, and convent, and they gave weekly alms. Bank and check records don't lie. The altar they were buried at was bought for the new church by them. They never worked under the table, and they voted every election. Republican or democrat didn't matter, they voted for the integrity of the candidate and whether they came for dinner or were good for business. They really voted for them; they catered to the legislature and were rewarded.

Mom passed a resolution for both houses of the legislature, and that tells how they appreciated her. The legislature was instrumental in backroom politics at the restaurant. It was led first by the best assemblyman Walter Kavanaugh, who then became state senator; his secretary, Ricky; Jack Penn and his significant other, Assemblyman

Alex DeCroce; Senators Dick Kamin, Robert Martin and Donald DeFrancesco: and later became Governor and Kip Bateman. Contracts for the state police union were instrumental, by the great Lieutenant Tommy Isrycki, the second father and honorary brother to the family, and at times, they worked into the wee hours of the night ironing differences, putting the dots, and commas, or sealing the deals. Then, they would get their materials and submit to the legislators and committees.

My job was server, cook, and at times, the look-out for the nosy people who would be wondering what we were doing all night. There was no hanky pranky. We were holier than thou. A secretary gave me the nickname of Crash because I was so tired I would crash my car, not into others but into the garage or a parked car, just trying to keep my eyes open. You had to be there. In my room is an American flag, given by the war department for her brother's service. That shows the sacrifice by my family in foreign wars and the patriotism for my family's adopted home of America. No one can deny our patriotism or our loyalty to these United States. God Bless America! Rest well, Mom and Dad. Your job on this earth is done and your destiny fulfilled. The years that go by will be the testament of our resolve and whether we have earned your trust, in not so much words and deeds, but in using the money you bequeathed to good projects, good people, and savings, which is so important and can be wasted frivolously. The goal is to live in harmony with our neighbors and be a good person, like you and Mom were to each other and to the community as a whole.

The End

Printed in the United States
by Baker & Taylor Publisher Services